W9-CCU-289

The Sneaky Chef to the Rescue

101 All-New Recipes and "Sneaky" Tricks for

Creating Healthy Meals Kids Will Love

BY MISSY CHASE LAPINE

RUNNING PRESS
PHILADELPHIA • LONDON

© 2009 by Missy Chase Lapine

All rights reserved under the Pan-American and International Copyright Conventions

Printed in China

This book may not be reproduced in whole or in part, in any form or by any means, electronic or mechanical, including photocopying, recording, or by any information storage and retrieval system now known or hereafter invented, without written permission from the publisher.

9   8   7   6   5   4   3

Digit on the right indicates the number of this printing

Library of Congress Control Number: 2008944145

ISBN 978-0-7624-3546-3

Cover design by Bill Jones and Kristopher Weber

The Sneaky Chef Logo by Kristopher Weber

Interior design by Alicia Freile

Edited by Jennifer Kasius

Cover photo and food photography by Jerry Errico

Food styling by Brian Preston-Campbell

Typography: Frutiger, Garth Graphic, Sassoon, Ardleys Hand, and Johnny Script

Running Press Book Publishers

2300 Chestnut Street

Philadelphia, PA 19103-4371

Visit us on the web!

www.runningpress.com

The ideas, methods, and suggestions contained in this book are not intended to replace the advice of a nutritionist, doctor, or other trained health professional. You should consult you pediatrician before adopting the methods of this book. Any additions to, or changes in diet, are at the reader's discretion.

I dedicate this book to my enthusiastic readers and their families.

Table of Contents

Chapter Four: Sneaky Chef Every Day 73

Breakfast Recipes:

Lunch Recipes:

Dinner and Side Recipes:

Treats and Drink Recipes:

Chapter Five: The Sneaky Chef Celebrates 197

Chapter Eight: Sneaky Chef Classics 275

Acknowledgments 290

Foreword

by Tyler Florence

Twelve years ago, when my first son, Miles, was born, it was not only one of the happiest days of my life but it was a day that changed the way I looked at cooking and food forever. I'd spent the better part of my young adult life cooking and eating my way through culinary school and the kitchens of New York City—but nothing prepared me for the challenges that would come when faced with the life-changing responsibility of feeding a child.

From my first days of fatherhood, I realized that the choices I made in how I fed Miles (and later, how I taught him to eat himself) were of the greatest importance and would surely play a big role in his becoming the happy, healthy young man he is today. It was then that I began work on a baby food line called Sprout, which is my way of helping parents not only nourish their babies but also educate their children's palates to appreciate natural, healthy foods that taste great too. A child's eating habits and preferences are established at a very early age and it is a parent's responsibility to ensure that what they learn about food in the very beginning will lead them to an adulthood of healthy eating. In the years since Miles was born, I've had a lot of time to work on my recipes and to try them out on my two newest little eaters, Hayden and Dorothy. The smiles on their faces as they try a delicious roasted pear puree is as rewarding as it gets.

When I first met Missy Chase Lapine, a.k.a. The Sneaky Chef, I was truly inspired by the work she has put into keeping kids and families healthy together. She's right. It's definitely not easy pushing the good stuff on kids, and it can take a little craftiness to make it happen. Her tried-and-true techniques are just what you need to make sure that your family is eating down the right path. But, no matter how sneaky you might get, if a dish doesn't pass the taste test, it's all for naught. *The Sneaky Chef to the Rescue* is filled with recipes that are fun, inventive, and most importantly, they are absolutely delicious. Give these recipes a try and I promise you, your family will thank you for it.

—Tyler Florence
Chef, Author & Founder of Sprout Foods

In Response to You

When I wrote my first book, *The Sneaky Chef*, I was inspired by my own experiences as a mom as well as those of my friends and neighbors. Mealtimes at my house were stressful showdowns between my kids and me over the food on their plate, and for a while, I felt cursed. Then I spoke to other moms and found that many of them had the same picky-eater problem. Each family was different, of course, because each kid's persnickety-ness was unique. Some children didn't like the food to touch (re: contaminate) other food on the plate. Some only ate foods of certain colors (one child I knew wouldn't eat anything that wasn't white). Others wouldn't even eat a *cookie* if it was broken, chipped, or otherwise damaged. Food that was first tasted by their younger sister? Forget about it. And topping the list of "no-way, no-how" foods: anything that was considered "good for you."

Among my friends and neighbors, it was generally accepted that having picky eaters was just one more challenge of parenting, akin to putting them to bed at night without incurring complaints, and getting them dressed for school with matching socks and all the right books in their backpack. We shrugged our shoulders and shared "amusing" stories about how our kids would inspect every inch of the plate to make sure there was nothing "funny" or "weird" about the meal. (In fact, one woman told me her son was so good at ferreting out an alien taste that she had named him her "food detective.")

What we didn't share with each other was how deeply it bothered us that our kids weren't getting the nutrients they needed. Their health was in our hands, and we were letting them down because we didn't know how to counter their irrational and unreasonable food aversions. Rather than trying to fight a losing battle against a kid making an "Ick!" face, we caved. People who didn't have kids just didn't understand. They would say things like, "Why don't you just *make* them eat it? You're the adult." And we would think, "You just cannot imagine how hard it is to make a child eat when he doesn't want to."

I had some notion that parents beyond my community must have picky eaters, but until I wrote my first book I had no idea how far-reaching the problem really was. As *The Sneaky Chef* hit the bookstores, I made appearances across the country and on national shows like the *Today Show*, *Fox & Friends*, *iVillage*, and more. That's when I realized I had struck one gigantic nerve. I was flooded with feedback: hundreds and hundreds of emails blinked in my inbox, bloggers took up the cause, and my friends and neighbors flagged me down to discuss the night's menu.

This book, in part, is an answer to all those parents who reached out to me. It not only expands your Sneaky Chef recipe repertoire but addresses tricky issues like cooking for kids with food allergies, helping kids who need to watch their weight do so without giving them a complex, and making special occasions happy *and* healthy.

Indeed, many of the letters from (mostly) mothers boiled down to the fact that parents saw only two options before them: berate their children into eating healthy or let them follow their own preferences and consume foods that were entirely wrong for their growing bodies. Some choice! As with my friends and me, these people hadn't been able to express how much they had been losing sleep over the issue until they discovered the solution *The Sneaky Chef* offered. "I have struggled with this for years," one woman wrote, "until I read your book. Thank you so much for showing me recipes that finally provide nutrition for my kids! They now eat veggies in nearly every meal without even knowing it. I finally have some peace of mind."

"If I could meet Missy I would give her the hugest hug. Because without this book I would definitely not have the kids I have today."

—Tina E., Australia (mum of six)

And whether we recognized it or not, the unhealthy diet we were letting our kids get away with was beginning to make us question ourselves as mothers. I received many emails that echoed this one: "I struggled for years to get my child to eat green vegetables. I couldn't stand the idea of letting her grow up without having a single salad. Feeding is an essential part of mothering, and finally—I feel like a good one."

Still, some have wondered if pulling a fast one on your kids is in the Good Parent Rule Book. Personally, I consider sneaking healthy ingredients into meals not only to be the ultimate magic trick when all other methods have failed, but one that should be performed with other approaches to enhance their effectiveness. What this means is that sneaking does not release us from the responsibility of serving fruits and vegetables or educating our kids about the value of a healthy diet. I suggest talking to kids about healthy food all the time; I just don't see any point in fighting about it. If the dinner table is a war zone, then the combatants won't listen—or learn—from each other. Once Mom and Dad know that the meal has spinach in it, they can wait and talk about the importance of leafy greens another time when the kids aren't fidgeting in their seats—or worse, digging in for an epic battle of wills.

A Little Bit of Heaven Blog

"The only way to make sneaking a way of life — and many readers told me that they now 'live from this book'—is if you can find a way to do it at almost every meal.

Children grow a little every day, so every day you have to give them the ammunition to grow strong and healthy. This cookbook is more of a guidebook than an everyday, every-meal, how-to manual for squeezing in nutrients whenever and wherever you can. That is the Sneaky Chef way. Whether you have a child who loves veggies outright or who won't let a carrot touch his lips, **The Sneaky Chef** will more than double your family's intake of healthy foods overnight.

Another wonderful aspect of **The Sneaky Chef** is that I still serve side dishes of veggies or fruit. I make them have at least a few bites of everything. And now that I know there is good stuff in the meal, I don't get worried about the couple of bites of green beans. This way my children can experience the textures and flavors of things a little at a time."

—Stephanie L., Buckeye, AZ (mother of 4)
(adapted from www.alittlebitofheaven.blogspot.com)

The subject of healthy eating should always be presented in a positive context, or the lessons won't sink in. I never harp on what "bad" foods do to us. For instance, I don't elaborate on the terrible side effects of French fries that are deep-fried in saturated fatty oil. This approach fails to make an impression at all, or it makes the wrong one—giving the fries an allure of the forbidden, er, fruit. Instead, my approach is almost entirely positive. I emphasize what they'll *get out of* the healthier foods. I tell my kids how much faster they'll run when they're playing soccer or how much smarter they'll be in math class. I tell them that while other kids are getting sick, they'll feel great because their immune system will fight off the germs. And that they'll probably spend less time in the dentist's chair.

After all, can you really afford to wait until your child is mature enough to understand *why* he should eat healthy food before you *feed him* the healthy food?

Once readers get the hang of sneaking, they seem to experience something like exhilaration when they realize they are actually getting away with it:

- "What a little gem this book is. I had to make brownies for my son's classroom party, and I didn't feel the least bit guilty since I knew they were getting a dose of spinach. In fact, I loved it that the kids didn't know!"

- "For the past two days, Elayna has eaten spaghetti and meatballs loaded with the Green Puree. She is actually eating spinach—and she begs me for it!"

- "I have never been so enthralled with a cookbook before this. It's especially good if you have kids who go through food jags— they frequently reject veggies they formerly loved. Now I have different veggie blends that hide in dishes he eats without complaint. I can't believe it works."

- "My family is blissfully unaware that they are eating yams, carrots, zucchini, cauliflower, and tofu. Every time I watch my daughter eat veggies with her eggs, I can hardly contain my giddiness. She has yet to turn down a dish!"

- "Every night for the past three weeks, I sit at the dinner table and smile as I watch my family eat things they would refuse if I served it to them outright. I didn't hide the idea that I am sneaking ingredients, but it's kind of a game. My kids say, 'Is this healthy for us Mom, because it sure tastes good?' Hee, hee!!!"

"I'm still loving your books, and it will be a long time before I've exhausted the ideas in them!"

—Mary-Belle S., Steley, NC (mother of 9)

"Are There Blueberries in My Juice?"

Dear Missy,

Our daughter, Jessica, was a five-year-old activist against the consumption of most fruits and vegetables. I bought several "kid-friendly" cookbooks, but the cucumber caterpillars and bogus broccoli trees never fooled her. She vehemently opposed certain foods with a resounding, "uh-uh." My little rebel didn't know what hit her when I introduced The Sneaky Chef in our home almost a year ago. After my first few weeks of using the book, she started asking, 'Are you cooking something from the Sneaky Chef book?' She liked the new recipes as long as they were within her comfort zone; hence Missy's ingenious theory, "Hiding Healthy Food in Kid's Favorite Meals."

I am envious of the puree critics who believe "Serve your kids healthy foods from the start and they will love them." Well, I did that. Vegetables and fruit have always been served on the plate and are in ready supply for snacks. I can't fathom what it would be like to hear my child say, "I'll have some broccoli" instead of, "Can I have that cupcake?" Since that doesn't appear to be a realistic expectation for Jessica, The Sneaky Chef is a creative, well-planned solution for increasing the nutritional value in the foods she will eat.

When first introducing food, we offered Jessica an expansive repertoire of raw, boiled, steamed, baked, and squashed fruits and veggies. She loved eating everything until she was about two and a half. Then Jessica began rejecting most foods, causing her daily caloric intake to dwindle. I mentioned the change in diet to the pediatrician. He said it was normal and she'd eat when she was hungry. The dinner battles quickly ensued.

My husband and I work full time, so meals with minimal prep time had to be the norm. The sides of fruits and veggies were garnished with sundry condiments to entice her. Whenever a new meal was offered, Jessica whined, "uh-uh," slouched in her chair, and crossed her arms in protest. It was tempting to give in and make something else for her to eat. However, we refused to add "short-order cooks" to our resumes.

Frustrated, we tried making Jessica sit at the table until she ate; she'd fall asleep before finishing. We sent her to her room until she felt like eating; she never felt like eating. We withheld snacks at school, believing they were too filling;

she felt isolated from her classmates, and she still didn't eat. Concerned we would be trading one bad eating habit for a lifelong eating disorder, we abandoned those practices.

Three years and countless lost battles later, we were at our wits' end. And never mind the ten- to fifteen-exposure rule—I've been at this for three years during a critical growth period in Jessica's life. Salvation appeared on the Today Show in the form of the Sneaky Chef. Missy claimed her recipes could fool the pickiest eater and the pièce de résistance was the Brainy Brownies. If she could sneak spinach into brownies and make them taste good, then I had to get a copy of that book!

All of the ingredients for the brownies were purchased in anticipation of using Missy's guide to a healthier kid. I thawed the blueberries and ate a few in front of Jessica, hoping she'd try one. No luck. I pulled out the "No Thank You Bite" rule (you have to try at least one bite) only to be met with a child who somehow avoided giving herself whiplash. With lips pursed and a nasally whimper emanating through her flaming nostrils, her head contorted to the left, then vigorously twisted to the right. My heart filled with doubt.

Despite my reservations, I made the spinach-laced brownies. Jessica had fallen asleep on the couch for her afternoon nap, so I woke her up for a "special treat." The sight of the powdered sugar-dusted brownies sent her into a fit of giggles. After two brownies, she asked, "Can I have another one?" Soon I was giddily running brownies around the neighborhood to fellow commiserators.

Grocery lists were based on Missy's recipes, and I logged onto her website almost nightly. I shared a lot of the food with friends and stocked my freezer with prepared meals. Everybody I had contact with heard about the Sneaky Chef (my apologies to the strangers I approached in the store, unsolicited). For months, my dear friends and family listened to me praise the Sneaky Chef. Even my husband thought I had gone mad with the scheming and conniving. But it didn't take long before I caught him dumping baby food into the spaghetti sauce!

The whole family is enjoying the healthier recipes with the increased nutrition. Emily, our two-year-old, is quickly approaching the age when Jessica became picky. We are more optimistic with Emily because she's already enjoying the sneaky meals and still likes fruits and vegetables. Dinners overall are more enjoyable, with time to talk about our day rather than repeating "EAT, Jessica," or "take one more bite, please."

—Sue R., Bethelem GA (mother of 2)

As a working mom, I know it's not always possible to whip up a batch of from-scratch brownies. That's why part of the Sneaky Chef philosophy is to help people make the most of the real lives they lead (as opposed to the imaginary ideal of a house that's always spotless, a job that's stress-free, and kids who always do exactly what you want). So it made my day when I received emails from people all over the country who described how easy it was to use *The Sneaky Chef*. "I made my first batch of purees the other day. I got six done in one hour during my son's nap time!" says one mom. Another wrote, "I just whipped up a batch of purees and froze them in one-cup quantities. Now, every time I open *The Sneaky Chef*, I just pop one out of the freezer and I'm good to go."

"I am a kitchen rock star!! The kids ASKED FOR SECONDS on dinner (I had a better chance of Brad Pitt calling me for a date before this happened!). The cookies are wonderful and I have been cackling wickedly with the knowledge that my children have finally met their match. As a result of what you have accomplished (no mother alive has been made happier since getting her first full night of sleep), we are discussing erecting a monument in your honor!"

—Chase M., Cape Elizabeth, ME (mother of 2)

A sneaky surprise has been that many parents told me their kids are "in on it and love it." There are still those kids, however, where sneaking can only be successful if you don't get caught. Either way, a recipe is only healthy if you can get your kids to actually eat your food, so I work hard in my test kitchen to create fail-safe recipes that you can count on every time. One *Sneaky Chef* reader, a mother of a two-year-old, had never cooked in her life. It was so bad that her child survived primarily on peanut butter and jelly sandwiches. Feeling adventurous, she bought my book and decided to make the baked ziti while her husband was at work. It was so easy that she tackled the sneaky brownies next. In the five years they'd been married, she had never so much as turned on the oven, so you can imagine how shocked her husband was to be served a steaming dish of pasta. And when she gave him fresh-baked brownies for dessert, he nearly fell out of his chair. She neglected to mention the vegetables she had snuck into both recipes.

For the next week, she made a new Sneaky Chef dinner every night. Finally, he asked where his wife had gone, "You know, the *real* wife." And then she came clean about the subterfuge. She told him about the sweet potatoes in the French toast and the cauliflower in the ziti. She confessed to the tofu in the lasagna and the broccoli in the meatloaf. The biggest betrayal, and the one she saved for last, was the blueberries in the brownies. He hated blueberries. She expected him to call poison control and turn her in, but instead, a sly smile spread across his face. "Sneaky," he said admiringly. "Very sneaky."

TIPS

Readers tell me that *The Sneaky Chef* is a book that they "live from," not just use. It formed the basis of a new way of feeding their families, and so naturally they made it their own. Using my methods, the philosophy, and the recipes as a springboard, readers discovered helpful and often ingenious tips for expanding the idea of sneaky cooking. Here are a few of the best ones:

• Add avocado and tofu to shakes
• Stir homemade fruit purees like cherry and strawberry into yogurt
• Add Orange Puree to peanut butter

The Best Contribution I Can Make to Their Overall Health

Dear Sneaky Chef,

I'm a child-care provider. And I love it. I'm a cultivator of happiness, education, and health in children. I love them and want the best for them. And there is nothing I love more than meal times with "my" kids.

I've read the argument against "deceiving" the children with sneaky ingredients. That argument doesn't make sense to me. I have never printed or recited an ingredient list for any child I've cooked for. I don't owe them an ingredient list; I owe them the best contribution I can make to their overall health. As an early childhood professional, I know that lifelong eating problems begin in these years. I can't imagine using bribery, coercion, withholding, or threats for "encouragement" of eating—and I can't imagine how one would get ingredients such as

whole-leaf spinach into some four-year-olds without these or other potentially damaging avenues. The children in my care are focused on learning through play and happy experiences. Once we establish a healthy attitude and a foundation of trust, a child is open to learning and trying more. I've found nutrition to be a shining example of this.

My worst case, without a doubt, was my seven-year-old stepson. He would literally panic and cry at the sight of "real" food put in front of him. Last summer, he was transformed within the first two weeks of his time in our home. Aside from anything sugar laden, he ate five things: hot dogs, chicken nuggets, pizza, macaroni and cheese, and—even one vegetable!—corn. I had my work cut out. Pizza and macaroni and cheese: We could easily work with those—Orange Puree. Chicken nuggets were not so easy to hide stuff in, but flax and wheat germ were stealth troopers. Over the course of our five-week summer visit, his attitude toward eating changed dramatically. He even ate—gasp—broccoli (without disguise). Of course, the Sneaky Chef was in the kitchen, but he never noticed her. She helped with desserts, primarily: puddings, sorbets, smoothies, muffins, and brownies.

I hide Sneaky purees and flours in something, every day. I'm responsible for 70 percent of my daycare children's daily nutrition; to me, this is a serious responsibility.

I think every school and child-care provider needs to implement some of the Sneaky Chef philosophy in their program. It doesn't take exquisite planning. It only takes some enthusiasm, understanding, and lots of love (aka Sneaky ingredients).

—Julia S., Murrieta, CA (child-care provider and mother of 5)

- Mix White Bean Puree into mayonnaise
- Stir the puree into all-liquid or semi-liquid condiments, and into guacamole
- Sneak wheat germ or oat bran into sauces
- Freeze vegetable puree in an ice cube tray so you can defrost and experiment with new recipes in a flash
- Use some of the vitamin-rich water you boiled vegetables in for purees and other dishes
- Use evaporated skim milk to replace cream in soups and sauces
- Substitute raw cane sugar or honey for white sugar
- Make Orange and White Purees in larger batches since they are used in so many recipes
- Add purees to frozen dinners (like the mashed potatoes)
- Add purees or juice to salad dressing to cut fat

WHAT'S NEW

Sneaky Chef to the Rescue has more than a hundred all-new recipes and gives you clever solutions to new food challenges submitted by readers. Plus, many readers asked for special attention to three areas, to which I've devoted three new chapters. The first one is called "Sneaky Chef Light." In it, I offer recipes that are deliberately low in fat and will be especially appealing to children and teenagers. It's a perfect way to give kids the food they need to maintain or lose weight without making them feel deprived or singled out.

The second special chapter is called "Sneaky Chef for Food Allergies." I was surprised at how many emails I received from parents whose loved ones had serious food allergies. Kids with allergies often feel deprived because they have to either give up everything they love or eat such a degraded version that it's not worth it. This chapter will delight them with delicious alternatives, dishes that don't taste "weird" or doctored. My recipes genuinely taste like the real thing, and kids will gobble them up.

The third special chapter is called "Sneaky Chef Celebrates": recipes for holidays, birthdays, and other special occasions. One issue readers complained about was that all their dedication and hard work at losing weight throughout the rest of the year was virtually obliterated between November and December. The recipes in this chapter cover many holiday favorites and are specifically designed to *taste unhealthy*—that is, fat-filled and delicious—even though they aren't. Another issue that has been elevated to the level of a national debate is potentially banning the humble cupcake from schools and bake sales. This chapter provides a simple solution to the cupcake conundrum.

I've made it my mission to help parents rescue the family meal from stress and strain, and reclaim the dinner table for health and happiness. After all, gathering around a table should be a time for the people you love best to share a few moments of their day. I wish you and your families a lifetime of such peaceful and healthy meals together.

The Sneaky Lists

Once you know something, you can't un-know it. Which is both good and bad. By gaining knowledge about nutritious, least-toxic foods, you are giving your family a head start on long, happy lives. But once you know a few things about nutrition, you can't wander aimlessly down the grocery aisles, picking out canned vegetables, boxed macaroni, and frozen dinners without a second thought. If you want to eat smart, you have to buy smart, and that begins with making informed choices.

There is an old adage: don't shop for groceries when you're hungry. (Your growling stomach will prompt you to buy far more food than you need.) To that I would add: don't shop without a list. It will keep you from impulse purchases (which are often packed with chemicals, fats, and sugars), from items you might need for dishes you'll never serve, and from leaving out items you actually will need—tonight.

The following lists will guide you in stocking your Sneaky Chef arsenal of good-for-you foods. This catalog covers every aisle in the grocery store (I suggest photocopying it and bringing it with you). Most items are grouped in such a way that you will find them sold in the same vicinity in the store, which will make shopping much more efficient, easy, and complete. And if you like to shop only once a week, we've provided a weekly menu planner for you to photocopy and take with you to the store as well.

THE TWELVE MOST IMPORTANT FOODS TO BUY ORGANIC

These are the fruits and vegetables to be watch out for because they've been designated by the USDA Pesticide Data Program as the *most* contaminated with pesticide residues. Whenever possible, choose the organic version of these to lessen your risk. The reason they carry more pesticides is that they have either thin skin or no skin at all, so you can't peel off the offending area and eat something pure. People who eat the nonorganic version on a regular basis are exposing themselves to more than twenty different pesticides per day. Yes, twenty. I've cataloged these foods from the *most to least* contaminated:

Peaches

Strawberries

Apples

Spinach

Nectarines

Celery

Pears

Cherries

Potatoes

Sweet bell peppers

Raspberries

Imported grapes

List Two:

THE TWELVE LEAST CONTAMINATED FOODS

Conversely, you can reduce your contact with pesticides by stocking up on the *least* contaminated foods, by USDA standards. Two other ways to keep food cleaner is to one, wash your hands before preparation and two, wash and peel the item when it's called for. (You might want to eat sweet peas whole.) Contrast the exposure of twenty pesticides a day on list 1 with this list, which exposes you to about two. Their thick skins (or natural casings) protect the part that you eat from sprayed pesticides. The list begins with the *least* contaminated:

Sweet corn

Avocados

Pineapples

Cauliflower

Mangoes

Sweet peas, shelled

Asparagus

Onions

Broccoli

Bananas

Kiwis

Papayas

List Three:

SNEAKY STAPLES TO KEEP IN THE KITCHEN

These are the staples I use throughout the recipes in this book. Having these items on hand makes it easier to whip up Sneaky Chef recipes for every meal. And if you're so inclined, you can easily find organic versions of many of these items.

PRODUCE:

☐ **Baby spinach**

☐ **Zucchini, *fresh***

☐ **Broccoli, *fresh***

☐ **Sweet potatoes (or yams)**

☐ **Cauliflower, *fresh***

☐ **Fresh berries, in season**

☐ **Bananas**

☐ **Avocados**

☐ **Onions**

☐ **Potatoes, russet**

☐ **Lemons**

MEAT/FISH:

☐ **Beef, lean ground**

☐ **Turkey, lean ground**

☐ **Hot dogs (no nitrates)**

☐ **Fish fillets—tilapia, or flounder**

☐ **Chicken—skinless, boneless tenders or drumsticks**

CEREALS/FLOUR:

☐ **Wheat germ, unsweetened**

☐ **Oat bran**

☐ **Rolled oats, old-fashioned, not quick-cooking**

☐ **Cereal, high-fiber flakes**

☐ **Cereal, brown rice**

- [ ] Flour, whole wheat (stone ground)
- [ ] Flour, white (unbleached)
- [ ] Cornmeal

RICE/PASTA:

- [ ] Brown rice
- [ ] Macaroni and cheese, boxed (ideally without artificial colors)
- [ ] Whole wheat pasta—elbows and ziti
- [ ] Wonton wrappers
- [ ] Lasagna noodles, "no boil"

BREAD:

- [ ] Bread, whole wheat
- [ ] Tortillas, whole wheat flour
- [ ] Tortillas, corn
- [ ] Bread crumbs, whole wheat
- [ ] Whole wheat pita bread, pocketless
- [ ] Bagels, whole wheat

CANNED GOODS:

- [ ] Garbanzo beans ("chickpeas")
- [ ] White beans ("butter beans," navy, or cannellini)
- [ ] Refried beans, low fat, vegetarian
- [ ] Baked beans, vegetarian
- [ ] Tomatoes, plum, whole
- [ ] Sardines, in water, skinless and boneless

- [ ] Tuna, in water (preferably "chunk light")
- [ ] Tomato paste
- [ ] Evaporated skim milk
- [ ] Tomato soup, ideally low-sodium

JARS/BOTTLES:

- [ ] Baby foods—especially sweet potatoes, carrots, peas, zucchini, garden vegetables, prunes, plums, apricots, blueberries, spinach, and broccoli
- [ ] Pomegranate juice
- [ ] Salsa
- [ ] Applesauce
- [ ] Ranch dressing (no MSG)
- [ ] Ketchup
- [ ] Pasta sauce

FROZEN FOODS:

- [ ] Blueberries, frozen (preferably without added syrup or sweeteners)
- [ ] Strawberries, frozen (preferably without added syrup or sweeteners)
- [ ] Cherries, frozen, pitted (preferably without added syrup or sweeteners)
- [ ] Green peas, sweet
- [ ] Corn, yellow, off cob
- [ ] Edamame (soybeans in shell)

NUTS/OILS:

☐ Almonds, blanched and slivered

☐ Extra-virgin olive oil, cold pressed

☐ Canola oil, cold pressed

☐ Cooking oil, spray

TEA/COCOA:

☐ Cocoa, unsweetened

☐ Green tea, decaffeinated

DESSERTS:

☐ Chocolate chips, semisweet

☐ Sprinkles, multicolored

☐ Jell-O, not premade

☐ Gelatin, unflavored

☐ Chocolate syrup

☐ Whipped cream, spray can

☐ Frozen yogurt, low-fat

DAIRY/EGGS:

☐ Yogurt, low-fat, plain

☐ Cheese, low-fat, shredded

☐ American cheese slices

☐ Ricotta cheese, low-fat

☐ Tofu, firm block

☐ Eggs (with added Omega-3)

☐ Parmesan cheese, grated

☐ Powdered milk, nonfat

OTHER:

☐ Chicken broth, boxed (no MSG), ideally low-sodium

☐ Vegetable broth, boxed (no MSG), ideally low-sodium

☐ Cinnamon

☐ Honey

☐ Pure maple syrup

☐ Pure vanilla extract

☐ Baking powder, nonaluminum

☐ Baking soda

☐ Powdered sugar

☐ Brown sugar

☐ Jam, no sugar added

☐ Lentils (dried or canned)

List Four:

THE SNEAKY CHEF'S FAVORITE TOOLS

There's nothing like a well-stocked kitchen to make cooking easier, faster, and more pleasant. Think of your kitchen shelves and drawers the same way you do your house— you don't have to decorate it all at once. Nor do you have to stock your kitchen with every conceivable device. Choose one piece at a time; make sure it's something you need and love in equal measures. Individual items might seem expensive, but the good stuff will last forever. If you prorate it at cost-per-day over a lifetime, it comes out to pennies. Not everyone can afford the upscale cooking stores (but do browse them for the sheer fun of it); try restaurant and hotel supply houses instead. These are where the pros go, and you know they can't be fooled. Good equipment is sturdy, efficient, and beautiful, and even if you aren't a chef, it will make you feel like one.

However, if you're not in a position to start buying spatulas, meat thermometers, and nonstick pans, fear not. You can still be a great Sneaky Chef. That's because my mission is changing the way America feeds its families, not turning everyone into a five-star chef! As long as you have the basics, you can still make every recipe in this book. Having said that, I would like to suggest the following handy tools to make your experience in the kitchen as enjoyable as possible (as well as to cut down on cooking time if you're a busy mom).

Mini food processor, 3-cup capacity

Donut pan

Muffin tins

Colander or strainer

Tongs (I'm a huge fan—I use them for everything)

A whisk

Parfait "ice cream" glasses

Straws

Popsicle molds

Rolling pin

Brownie or cake pan

Kitchen shears (amazingly handy—you can cut fat off meat, slice a pizza, give your kid a haircut)

Handheld stick blender (use directly in the soup pan to puree while it's still on the burner)

Regular blender (great for smoothies)

Sharp chef's knife (even if you only have one knife, make it a good one)

Cookie/baking sheet

Measuring spoons and cups

Parchment paper

Plastic bags

Sneak Chef Meal Planner

	BREAKFAST	LUNCH	DINNER	TREAT	PUREE TO MAKE THIS WEEK
Monday					
Tuesday					
Wednesday					
Thursday					
Friday					
Saturday					
Sunday					

MEAL PLANNING TIPS:

- Try a new fruit or veggie every week
- Make meals once, then use leftovers in another form the next day (e.g., meat sauce one day, cheeseburger stuffed potatoes the next day)
- Choose one puree a day and make all recipes using that puree
- Make several batches of purees ahead— one time per week; store in the refrigerator for three days or freezer for three months
- Clean and chop veggies and store in plastic bags for a few days so they are ready to use

List Five:
THE SNEAKY CHEF'S BAG OF TRICKS

New to the sneaky scene? There are thirteen "methods of disguise" in the Sneaky Chef's Bag of Tricks. (These methods are summarized here, but are described in full detail in my first book, *The Sneaky Chef: Simple Strategies for Hiding Healthy Foods in Kids' Favorite Meals*). The most commonly employed methods involve camouflage (blend in a puree), distraction (they'll notice the sprinkles but not the veggie taste), and some devious thinking (packing meals with a nutritious punch). This book expands on the classic *Sneaky Chef* methods and adds some new ones, too. With these ruses up your sleeve, your children's meals will disappear like magic!

Method One:
PUREE

Use a blender (best for liquids or already mushy solids, like smoothies, ice drinks, and soups) or a food processor (for whole fruits and vegetables that don't need a lot of added liquid) to puree food until it is silky smooth in texture and has the consistency of mashed potatoes. Pureeing makes food extremely nutrient-dense, which means your child is actually eating quite a bit when you sneak in even seemingly small amounts.

Method Two:
COMBINE REFINED AND UNREFINED

Using a combination of flours and whole grain will help you retain a good deal of a recipe's familiar texture and weight while still imparting substantial health benefits such as fiber, vitamins, and minerals. The flour blend called for in this book is always one-third white flour, one-third whole wheat, and one-third wheat germ—a mix that retains many of the properties of the original white flour.

Method Three:
USE FOODS THAT HIDE WELL

The real secret to being a Sneaky Chef is to hide the foods you don't want your kids to know they're eating. Just remember: hide ingredients in foods that are similar in color and texture; the healthy ingredient you use has to either enhance the overall original taste or add no taste of its own; avoid affecting the overall look or texture of the final product; and if you add something, it should be good for you.

Method Four:
SUBSTITUTE NUTRITIOUS LIQUID FOR WATER WHEN BOILING FOODS

You don't want to pass up *any* opportunity to sneak nutrition into your children's meals, so swap water in favor of liquids that enhance the nutritional value of the dish and complement its taste. Think: juices, milk, broth, and even decaffeinated green tea.

Method Five:

COMBINE FOODS THAT ARE A SPECIFIC NUTRITIONAL COMPLEMENT FOR EACH OTHER

Many of the recipes in this book are designed to combine ingredients that either form a more complete protein or help your body absorb nutrients. The trick? Disguise the combinations so that even if your kids only eat one dish, they'll receive the same benefit as eating from several platters. Plus, fewer dishes to wash!

Method Six:

IDENTIFY FOODS KIDS ARE LIKELY TO ENJOY STRAIGHT UP

There *are* healthy foods that kids will eat without any arm-twisting—like whole artichokes, popcorn, grapes, baby carrots, and corn on the cob. So serve them as much of these as you can, but know that they'll be better received if your kids are hungry and there aren't any junky snacks in sight. Introduce different foods when they're distracted or let them see you enjoy the food yourself—without offering them any. You'll be surprised how soon they'll be begging for a bite.

Method Seven:

ALTER THE COOKING METHOD TO AVOID FRYING

Choose steaming, baking, broiling, roasting, or grilling over frying. And when you do use oil, there are ways to keep it to a minimum: measure oil with a teaspoon or baste the oil with a pastry brush instead of pouring it from the bottle; blast the dish with high heat under the broiler for a minute to crisp the breading; use juice or broth to give a recipe the moistness it needs to mimic fattier foods. You'll get deep flavor without the deep fryer.

Method Eight:

CUT THE EFFECTS OF TOXINS OR FATS BY DILUTING THE INGREDIENTS WITH SOMETHING HEALTHIER

If your kids crave a certain unhealthy food, you can minimize its negative effects by diluting it with something that *is* good for them. Mix in a dose of sardines to reduce the mercury levels in tuna fish sandwiches; cut creamy salad dressings with plain yogurt; swap some of the butter in baked goods with fruit or vegetable puree. Once you figure out how to retain enough of the original flavor, your ideas may be the only thing that will remain undiluted!

Method Nine:

CUT CALORIES AND DOUBLE VOLUME WITH LOW-CAL, NUTRITIOUS "FILLERS"

This method adds volume to calorie-dense foods with nutritious ingredients that have fewer calories per portion, like mixing vegetable purees in mac 'n' cheese. By "bulking up" the dish, you feel more satisfied with fewer calories. Ingredients that have high water and fiber content—fruits and vegetables—work best.

Method Ten:

USE SLOWER-BURNING FOODS TO AVOID BLOOD SUGAR "SPIKE AND CRASH"

Foods that are high in sugar cause your blood sugar levels to rise quickly. This spike is followed by a corresponding quick drop, which leaves you with a distinct sense of energy depletion. Children seem especially susceptible to this phenomenon. Refined sugars and carbohydrates like white bread and pasta are the worst culprits. Swap them with complex carbs like whole grains and slow-burning proteins like beans and legumes. When you can't lose the spike-inducers, take the edge off by mixing in some good-for-you Steady Eddies.

Method Eleven:

USE *VISUAL* DECOYS TO MAKE FOOD LOOK APPEALING AND FUN

Divert your kids' attention away from the fact that the food you're serving them is actually healthy by using appealing colors, shapes, and sizes to your advantage. Dust powdered sugar onto good-for-you baked goods. Make things in miniature. Shape food with cookie cutters. Squirt whipped cream on, well, anything. Bottom line: looks are everything!

Method Twelve:

USE KID-FRIENDLY FLAVOR DECOYS TO DISTRACT KIDS FROM WHAT'S UNDERNEATH

Method Thirteen:

USE KID-FRIENDLY *TEXTURE* DECOYS

Make sure the taste doesn't give your sneak-iness away: use bold flavors that you know your kids already love. Use chocolate chips, cheese, ketchup, cocoa, ranch dressing. Did I mention ketchup? It's worth saying twice. Strong flavors deceive the taste buds and distract your child from picking up on any new flavors.

Something may look and taste great, but if it is lumpy or gritty or leafy, kids won't go anywhere near it. Change an objectionable texture in a recipe by adding ones kids love. Sprinkles, chocolate chips, cheese, crushed cereal toppings, raisins—all make good decoys.

Make-Ahead Recipes and Glossary of Superfoods

You can't be Sneaky without having something to hide. The following easy-to-make recipes are quite literally the hidden secrets of Sneaky Chef dishes. While they are undetectable, they pack a nutritional punch in every meal—after all, they're made from the world's best superfoods. First, refer to the Sneaky Lists chapter, starting on page 27, for the essential ingredients so you can stock your pantry ahead of time. Choose which recipes you want to make, see which Make-Aheads they call for, and you'll be primed to become an expert and virtually effortless Sneaky Chef.

Not only are these Make-Aheads the backbone of my recipes, but you can even add them to the Quick Fix recipes, ensuring that meal-in-a-box foods will also be spiked with healthy ingredients. (The Sneaky Chef never passes up a chance to upgrade meals with something fresh.) As you've probably discovered, it's a lot easier to ride the horse in the direction it's already going than to try and force it in another, even if the direction is toward less-than-perfect foods. The Quick Fixes keep you from having to fight your kids' taste. Let them eat the boxed mac 'n' cheese they insist on but slip in some Orange Puree, and you'll both be happy.

The Make-Aheads won't keep you in the kitchen for long. Just schedule a little extra time one afternoon a week to make the ones you'll be using later. Most of the recipes in this chapter only take about ten minutes to whip up. If you have a food processor, it's as simple as pressing a button. My personal favorites are the 3-cup miniprocessors (available on my website: www.TheSneakyChef.com). They're relatively inexpensive, easy to operate, and don't take up a lot of space. These minis work extremely well with the small amounts of ingredients we use in these Make-Aheads. This doesn't mean, however, that you can't use this book if you don't have a miniprocessor—a full-size processor or a blender will do the trick, although you may have to put in a little more liquid.

All of the following purees and juices can be stored in the refrigerator for up to three days and in the freezer for up to three months. It's easy to store them in quarter-cup sizes so you'll be at the ready whenever you're feeling sneaky.

Make-Ahead Recipe #1: Purple Puree

3 cups raw baby spinach
   leaves*

1½ cups fresh or frozen
   blueberries, no syrup
   or sugar added

½ teaspoon lemon juice

1 to 2 tablespoons water

Note: I prefer raw baby spinach to frozen spinach for this recipe (milder flavor); if you must use frozen spinach, only use 1 cup of it.

Raw baby spinach should be well rinsed, even if the package says "prewashed." If you're using frozen blueberries, give them a quick rinse under cold water to thaw a little, and then drain.

Place the spinach in the food processor and pulse a few times. This will reduce the spinach significantly. Next add the blueberries, lemon juice, and 1 tablespoon of water; puree on high until as smooth as possible. Stop occasionally to push the contents to the bottom. If necessary, use another tablespoon of water to create a smooth puree.

This recipe makes about 1 cup of puree; double it if you want to store another cup. It will keep in the refrigerator up to 3 days, or you can freeze ¼-cup portions in sealed plastic bags or small plastic containers.

PER SERVING (1 CUP, 310G): *Calories 145; Total Fat 1.1g; Fiber 7.2g; Total Carbohydrates 35.0g; Sugars 22.1g; Protein 4.2g; Sodium 73mg; Cholesterol 0mg; Calcium 102mg.*

Purple Puree is used in the following recipes:

Quick Fixes for Boxed Pancake Mix

Fudge Scones

Tijuana Lasagna

Quick Fix for Chocolate Cake Mix

Candy Cane Biscotti

Light Brainy Brownies

Gluten-Free Brownies

Eggless Brainy Brownies

Brainy Brownies

Make-Ahead Recipe #2: Orange Puree

1 medium sweet potato
   or yam, peeled and
   coarsely chopped
3 medium to large carrots,
   peeled and sliced into
   thick chunks
2 to 3 tablespoons water

PER SERVING (2 CUPS, 346G):
*Calories 200; Total Fat 0.6g;
Fiber 9.9g; Total Carbohydrates
46.8g; Sugars 15.2g; Protein
4.0g; Sodium 220mg, Cholesterol
0mg; Calcium 110mg.*

Place the sweet potatoes and carrots in a medium-sized pot and cover with cold water. Bring to a boil and cook for about 20 minutes, until carrots are very tender. Careful—if the carrots aren't tender enough, they may leave telltale little nuggets of vegetables in recipes, which will reveal their presence.

Drain the carrots and sweet potatoes and put them in the food processor with 2 tablespoons of water. Puree on high until smooth—no pieces of vegetables showing. Stop occasionally to push the contents to the bottom. If necessary, use another tablespoon of water to smooth out the puree, but the less water the better.

This recipe makes about 2 cups of puree; double it if you want to store more. Orange Puree will keep in the refrigerator for up to 3 days, or you can freeze ¼-cup portions in sealed plastic bags or small plastic containers.

"They actually eat more when I use the purees in their dishes and sandwiches than without them. You just have to plan ahead a little and decide what you want to feed them."

—Al P., Birmingham, AL (stay-at-home dad of triplets)

Orange Puree is used in the following recipes:

Peanut Better Waffles

Quick Fixes for Boxed Pancake Mix

French Toast Rollers

Breakfast Banana Bread Pudding

Monkey Bars

Monkey Pancakes

Sneaky "Bonbons"

Grilled Cheese and Tomato Soup

Portable Pizza Muffins

Sneak-wiches

Sneak 'n' Slice Pizza Bites

McSneaky Muffin—Mac 'n' Cheese Flavor

McSneaky Mexican Muffins

Honey Battered Popcorn Shrimp

Quick Fixes for Canned Soup

Tijuana Lasagna

Enlightened Enchiladas

Macaroni 'n' Beef Skillet

Sweet 'n' Sassy Meatballs

Sweet 'n' Sassy Sauce

Down Under BBQ Sauce

Slow Cooker Pulled BBQ Chicken

Quick Fix for Yellow Cake Mix

Roasted Squash Soup for the Holidays

Peanut Butter Blondies

Sammy's Pumpkin Spice Donuts
   (or Muffins)

Soufflé Surprise for Thanksgiving

Gingerbread Men for the Holidays

Bountiful Pumpkin Pie

Gluten-Free Chicken Tenders

Gluten-Free Pizza

Gluten-Free Peanut Butter Cookies

Eggless Banana Pancakes from
   Boxed Mix

Quick Fixes for Store-Bought
   Tomato Sauce

Crunchy Chicken Tenders

Quick Fixes for Peanut Butter

Quick Fixes for Boxed Mac 'n' Cheese

Make-Ahead Recipe #3: Green Puree

2 cups raw baby spinach
   leaves*

2 cups broccoli florets,
   fresh or frozen

1 cup sweet green peas,
   frozen

2 to 3 tablespoons water

*Note: I prefer raw baby
spinach to frozen spinach for
this recipe (milder flavor); if
you must use frozen spinach,
only use 1 cup of it.*

Raw baby spinach should be well rinsed, even if the package says "prewashed."

To prepare Green Puree on the stovetop, pour about 2 inches of water into a pot with a tight-fitting lid. Put a vegetable steamer basket into the pot, add the broccoli, and steam for about 10 minutes, until very tender. Add the frozen peas to the basket for the last 2 minutes of steaming. Drain.

To prepare in the microwave, place the broccoli in a microwave-safe bowl, cover with water, and microwave on high for 8 to 10 minutes, until very tender. Add the peas for the last 2 minutes of cooking. Drain.

Place the spinach in the food processor first and pulse a few times. This will reduce the spinach significantly. Next add the cooked broccoli and peas, along with 2 tablespoons of water. Puree on high until as smooth as possible. Stop occasionally to push the contents to the bottom. If necessary, use another tablespoon of water to make a smooth puree.

This recipe makes about 2 cups of puree; double it if you want to store more. Green Puree will keep in the refrigerator for up to 3 days, or you can freeze ¼-cup portions in sealed plastic bags or small plastic containers.

PER SERVING (2 CUPS, 392G): *Calories 211; Total Fat 1.3g; Fiber 14.9g; Total Carbohydrates 39.7g; Sugars 13.0g; Protein 15.4g; Sodium 112mg; Cholesterol 0mg; Calcium 188mg.*

"I'd like to use more raw vegetables without steaming
or cooking first in order to retain more nutrition.
Can I make your purees without cooking?"

—Bea M., Dallas, OR (mother of 2)

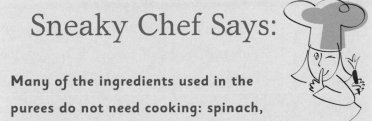

Sneaky Chef Says:

Many of the ingredients used in the purees do not need cooking: spinach, peas, blueberries, strawberries, and zucchini can all be used raw. But the cauliflower, broccoli, carrots, and yams do need to cook until tender in order to produce a smooth puree.

Green Puree is used in the following recipes:

Quick Fixes for Canned Soup

Sneak-wiches

Hamburger-Stuffed Potatoes

Enlightened Enchiladas

Speedy Stovetop Lasagna

Sneaky Sliders

Wizard's Wonton Soup

Italian Wedding Soup

Light Green Goddess Dressing

Make-Ahead Recipe #4: White Puree

2 cups cauliflower florets
(about half a small head)

2 small to medium zucchini,
peeled and coarsely
chopped

1 teaspoon fresh lemon
juice

1 to 2 tablespoons water,
if necessary

To prepare White Puree on the stovetop, pour about 2 inches of water into a pot with a tight-fitting lid. Put a vegetable steamer basket into the pot, add the cauliflower, and steam for about 10 minutes, until very tender. Drain.

To prepare in the microwave, place the cauliflower in a microwave-safe bowl, cover it with water, and microwave on high for 8 to 10 minutes or until very tender. Drain.

Meanwhile, place the raw peeled zucchini with the lemon juice in your food processor and pulse a few times. Next add the cooked cauliflower and 1 tablespoon of water to the food processor (work in batches if necessary) and puree on high until smooth. Stop occasionally to push the contents to the bottom. If necessary, use another tablespoon of water make a smooth puree, but the less water the better.

This recipe makes about 2 cups of puree; double it if you want to store more. It will keep in the refrigerator for up to 3 days, or you can freeze ¼-cup portions in sealed plastic bags or small plastic containers.

PER SERVING (1 CUP, 298G): *Calories 56; Total Fat 0.5g; Fiber 4.7g; Total Carbohydrates 12.1g; Sugars 5.9g; Protein 4.4g; Sodium 49mg; Cholesterol 0mg; Calcium 108mg.*

"I have a lot of yellow summer squash coming out of my garden.

Can I use this in the White or Orange purees?"

—Jennifer B., Owensboro, KY (mother of 4)

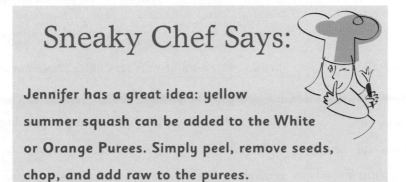

Sneaky Chef Says:

Jennifer has a great idea: yellow summer squash can be added to the White or Orange Purees. Simply peel, remove seeds, chop, and add raw to the purees.

White Puree is used in the following recipes:

Lunch Box Biscuits

Grilled Cheese and Tomato Soup

Quick Fixes for Canned Soup

Sneak 'n' Slice Pizza Bites

McSneaky Mexican Muffins

Tijuana Lasagna

Enlightened Enchiladas

Surprise Cheese Fries

Macaroni 'n' Beef Skillet

Olympic Fried Rice

Lucky Lo Mein

Slow Cooker Pulled BBQ Chicken

Down Under BBQ Sauce

Treasure-Stuffed Shells

Retro Tuna Casserole

Garlic Mashed Potatoes and Gravy
   for Thanksgiving

Holiday Green Bean Casserole

Light Mac 'n' Cheese

Clever Chicken Teriyaki

Gluten-Free Pizza

Quick Fixes for Boxed Mac 'n' Cheese

Quick Fixes for Store-Bought
   Tomato Sauce

Make-Ahead Recipe #5: Lentil Puree

⅔ cup lentils* (about 4
   ounces), rinsed

2 tablespoons water

*Green lentils have the
most fiber, but you can use
almost any color lentil for
this recipe—green, brown,
orange, black; also feel free
to substitute canned lentils
and skip the cooking step—
go right to pureeing.

Combine the lentils and 2 cups of water in a saucepan over
medium-high heat. Bring to a simmer, cover, and simmer for 35 to
40 minutes, or until lentils are tender. Drain any excess liquid and
fill the bowl of your food processor with the lentils and 1 tablespoon
of water. Puree on high until as smooth as possible, adding another
tablespoon of water if needed. Stop occasionally to push the
contents to the bottom. If necessary, use another tablespoon of
water to smooth out the puree.

This recipe makes about 1½ cups of puree; double it if you
want to store more. It will keep in the refrigerator up to 3 days,
or you can freeze ¼-cup portions in sealed plastic bags or small
plastic containers.

PER SERVING (1.5 CUPS, 602G): *Calories 452; Total Fat 1.4g; Fiber 39.1g;
Total Carbohydrates 76.9g; Sugars 2.6g; Protein 33.0g; Sodium 17mg; Cholesterol
0mg; Calcium 81mg.*

Lentil Puree is used in the following recipes:

Sneaky Sliders

Macaroni 'n' Beef Skillet

Mexican Cheeseburgers

Sneaky Gravy

Make-Ahead Recipe #6: Strawberry Puree

2½ cups fresh or frozen
  strawberries,* no syrup
  or sugar added

1 to 2 tablespoons water

*Try to use organic
strawberries, since they
rank high on the "dirty
dozen" list of produce
most contaminated with
pesticide residues.*

Fill the bowl of your food processor with the strawberries, lemon juice, and 1 tablespoon of water; puree on high until as smooth as possible. Stop occasionally to push the contents to the bottom. If necessary, use another tablespoon of water to smooth out the puree.

This recipe makes about 1 cup of puree; double it if you want to store another cup. It will keep in the refrigerator up to 3 days, or you can freeze ¼-cup portions in sealed plastic bags or small plastic containers.

PER SERVING (1 CUP, 377G): *Calories 115; Total Fat 1.1g; Fiber 7.2g; Total Carbohydrates 27.9g; Sugars 16.8g; Protein 2.4g; Sodium 3mg; Cholesterol 0mg; Calcium 58mg.*

Strawberry Puree is used in the following recipes:

Strawberry-Vanilla Breakfast Cookies

Chocolate Egg Cream

Christmas Morning Smoothies

Make-Ahead Recipe #7: Cherry Puree

2½ cups fresh or frozen
    cherries,* no syrup or
    sugar added
1 to 2 tablespoons water

Try to use organic cherries, since they rank high on the "dirty dozen" list of produce most contaminated with pesticide residues.

Fill the bowl of your food processor with the cherries, lemon juice, and 1 tablespoon of water; puree on high until as smooth as possible. Stop occasionally to push the contents to the bottom. If necessary, use another tablespoon of water to smooth out the puree.

This recipe makes about 1 cup of puree; double it if you want to store another cup. It will keep in the refrigerator up to 3 days, or you can freeze ¼-cup portions in sealed plastic bags or small plastic containers.

PER SERVING (1 CUP, 365G): *Calories 229; Total Fat 0.7g; Fiber 7.6g; Total Carbohydrates 58.3g; Sugars 46.5g; Protein 3.9g; Sodium 0mg; Cholesterol 0mg; Calcium 47mg.*

Cherry Puree is used in the following recipes:

French Toast Rollers

Hot Cocoa Oatmeal

Sneak-wiches

Slow Cooker Purple Chicken

Chocolate Egg Cream

Valentine's Day Red Smoothie

Pretty Pink Popcorn Balls for Valentines

Make-Ahead Recipe #8: Chickpea Puree

1 (15-ounce) can chickpeas*
(garbanzo beans)

2 to 3 tablespoons water

If you prefer to use dried beans, soak overnight and cook as directed

Rinse and drain the chickpeas and place them in the bowl of your food processor. Add 1 tablespoon of water, then pulse on high until you have a smooth puree. If necessary, use a little more water, a tiny bit at a time, until the mixture smoothes out and no pieces or full chickpeas are visible.

This recipe makes about 1 cup of puree; double it if you want to store another cup. It will keep in the refrigerator for up to 3 days, or you can freeze ¼-cup portions in sealed plastic bags or small plastic containers.

PER SERVING (1 CUP, 454G): *Calories 506; Total Fat 4.8g; Fiber 18.7g; Total Carbohydrates 96.2g; Sugars 0g; Protein 21.1g; Sodium 1272mg, Cholesterol 0mg; Calcium 137mg.*

Chickpea Puree is used in the following recipe:

Gluten-Free Pizza Crust

Make-Ahead Recipe #9: White Bean Puree

1 (15-ounce) can white beans* (Great Northern, navy, butter, or cannellini)

1 to 2 tablespoons water

If you prefer to use dried beans, soak overnight and cook as directed

Rinse and drain the beans and place them in the bowl of your food processor. Add 1 tablespoon of the water, then pulse on high until you have a smooth puree. If necessary, use a little more water, a tiny bit at a time, until the mixture smoothes out and no pieces or full beans are visible.

This recipe makes about 1 cup of puree; double it if you want to store another cup. It will keep in the refrigerator for up to 3 days, or you can freeze ¼-cup portions in sealed plastic bags or small plastic containers.

PER SERVING (1 CUP, 497G): *Calories 497; Total Fat 1.2g; Fiber 20.4g; Total Carbohydrates 93.3g; Sugars 0g; Protein 30.9g; Sodium 21mg, Cholesterol 0mg; Calcium 311mg.*

"I purchased this book because I needed more nutrition in a small amount of food. Boy, did I get more than I bargained for!"

—Elizabeth M., North Hills, CA

White Bean Puree is used in the following recipes:

Grandma Betty's Cornflake and
    Cheese Pudding

Inside-Out Snow Day French Toast

Bacon, Egg, and Cheese Breakfast
    Sticks

Cinnamon-Raisin Breakfast Cookies

Sammy's Scones

Pasta with Better Butter Sauce

Elmwood's Tuna Elbows

Grilled Cheese and Tomato Soup

Quick Fixes for Canned Soup

Sneak-wiches

Mighty Tots

Tater Pups

Quick Fix for Yellow Cake Mix

Cravin' Coffee Cake

Chanukah Latkes

Racy Rice Pudding

Brilliant Blondies

Santa's Sugar Cookies

Light Chocolate Chip Cookies

Quick Fixes for Peanut Butter

Light Sugar Cookies

Gluten-Free Chocolate Chip Cookies

Eggless and Nutless Chocolate Chip
    Cookies

Egg-Free, Dairy-Free, Gluten-Free
    Grits Sticks

Quick Fixes for Boxed Mac 'n' Cheese

Quick Fixes for Store-Bought
    Tomato Sauce

Unbelievable Chocolate Chip Cookies

Make-Ahead Recipe #10: Flour Blend*

1 cup all-purpose,
  unbleached white flour

1 cup whole wheat flour

1 cup wheat germ,
  unsweetened

Combine the flours and wheat germ in a large bowl. This makes about 3 cups. This blend can be stored in a sealed, labeled plastic bag or container in the refrigerator for up to 3 months.

*For Gluten-Free Flour Blend, see page 248.

Sneaky Tip:

A quick replacement for my Flour Blend is whole-grain "pastry" flour. It's still whole grain, but very finely milled for better taste, color, and texture.

PER SERVING (3 CUPS, 360G): *Calories1275; Total Fat 14.6g; Fiber 33.2g; Total Carbohydrates242g; Sugars 0.8g; Protein 56g; Sodium 22mg, Cholesterol 0mg; Calcium 104mg.*

Flour Blend is used in the following recipes:

Peanut Better Waffles

Bacon, Egg, and Cheese Breakfast
  Squares

Monkey Pancakes

Strawberry-Vanilla Breakfast Cookies

Gingerbread Men for the Holidays

Cinnamon-Raisin Breakfast Cookies

Sammy's Scones

Fudge Scones

Mom's Barley Breakfast Bars

Lunch Box Biscuits

Portable Pizza Muffins

Monkey Bars

Peanut Butter Blondies

Cravin' Coffee Cake

Brilliant Blondies

Sammy's Pumpkin-Spice Donuts
(or Muffins)

Holiday Pie Crust

Candy Cane Biscotti

Soufflé Surprise for Thanksgiving

Light Brainy Brownies

Santa's Sugar Cookies

Light Chocolate Chip Cookies

Light Sugar Cookies

Eggless and Nutless Chocolate Chip
Cookies

Eggless Pancakes

Eggless Brainy Brownies

Brainy Brownies

Unbelievable Chocolate Chip Cookies

"I have started using the Flour Blend when making

waffles or pancakes and no one is the wiser. My wife

even likes it! I also use it in my pizza dough recipes."

—Al P., Birmingham, AL (stay-at-home dad of triplets)

Make-Ahead Recipe #11: Ground Almonds

1 cup almonds, slivered and blanched

Pulse the almonds in a food processor. Don't let the food processor run continually, or you will end up with nut butter. You are aiming for a fairly coarse consistency.

This makes about ⅔-cup of ground almonds. Keep refrigerated in a sealed, labeled plastic bag for up to 2 weeks.

PER SERVING (⅔ CUP, 375G): *Calories 823; Total Fat 72.9g; Fiber 16.3g; Total Carbohydrates 26.6g; Sugars 6.8g; Protein 30.5g; Sodium 467mg; Cholesterol 0mg; Calcium 380mg.*

Ground Almonds are used in the following recipes:

Gluten-Free Pancakes

Egg-Free, Dairy-Free, Gluten-Free Granola Bars

Make-Ahead Recipe #12: Better Breading*

1 cup almonds, slivered
  and blanched (optional;
  omit if allergic)

1 cup bread crumbs,
  preferably whole wheat*

1 cup wheat germ,
  unsweetened

1 teaspoon salt

PER SERVING (1 CUP, 76G):
*Calories 442; Total Fat 4.0g;
Fiber 9.0g; Total Carbohydrates
94g; Sugars 1.0g; Protein 10.0g;
Sodium 43mg; Cholesterol 0mg.*

Pulse the almonds in a food processor. Don't let the food processor run continually, or you'll end up with nut butter. Pour the ground almonds into a plastic bag, and then add the bread crumbs, wheat germ, and salt. Seal and refrigerate up to 2 weeks.

For Gluten-Free Better Breading, see page 249.

Sneaky Tip:

Whole wheat bread crumbs can be found in natural and organic food stores, but you can easily make your own by pulsing whole-grain bread in a food processor to achieve fine crumbs. It's that simple. Three slices of bread yield about one cup of fresh crumbs. They keep for weeks in a sealed bag in the freezer.

Better Breading is used in the following recipe:

Crunchy Chicken Tenders

Make-Ahead Recipe #13: Ground Walnuts

1 cup shelled walnut
halves or pieces

Pulse the walnuts in a food processor. Don't let the food processor run continually, or you will end up with nut butter. You are aiming for a fairly coarse consistency.

This makes about ⅔- cup of ground walnuts. Keep refrigerated in a sealed, labeled plastic bag for up to 2 weeks.

PER SERVING (⅓ CUP, 125G): *Calories 772; Total Fat 73.8g; Fiber 8.5g; Total Carbohydrates 12.4g; Sugars 1.4g; Protein 30.1g; Sodium 2mg; Cholesterol 0mg; Calcium 76mg.*

Ground Walnuts are used in the following recipes:

Soufflé Surprise for Thanksgiving

Holiday Pie Crust

"The question I had is about sneaky in the purees using baby food, since I am often pressed for time. I like your suggestion to use it, but don't know if I should use the same amount. What are the quantities of baby food I should be substituting for your homemade purees?"

—Fran M. Island Park, NY (mother of 1)

Sneaky Chef Says:

Good question! You should use the exact same amount of baby food as the homemade puree called for in a recipe. For example, if my recipe calls for ½ cup of Orange Puree, use ¼ cup of baby food carrots and ¼ cup of baby food sweet potatoes.

Instant Supermarket Purees:

Note: Some Make-Aheads are actually unwittingly prepared for you by the food industry. If you find yourself short on time, or if you're in the midst of a recipe and you don't have a Make-Ahead on hand, some purees used in this book (although not all) can be substituted with baby foods.

MAKE AHEAD	INGREDIENTS	INSTANT SUBSTITUTE
White Puree	cauliflower, zucchini	baby food zucchini
Orange Puree	sweet potatoes, carrots	baby food sweet potatoes and carrots
Green Puree	peas, broccoli, spinach	baby food peas, mixed vegetables
Purple Puree	blueberries, spinach	baby food apples and blueberries
White Bean Puree	white beans	vegetarian refried pinto beans (these are darker in color and not as bland as white beans—they would work only with darker-colored meat and tomato sauce)
Lentil Puree		canned lentils
Cherry Puree		baby food apples and blueberries
Flour Blend		Whole-grain pastry flour

Sneaky Tip:

Other useful instant supermarket purees are tomato paste, applesauce, unsweetened fruit spread, and fresh, ripe avocados (mashed).

Host a Sneaky Chef Party!

Want to have fun with your friends while you're doing something healthy for everyone's family? Gather a group of sneaky conspirators, serve some snacks (healthy ones, of course), put on some music, and combine forces to whip up a whole month's supply of Sneaky Chef purees. Each person takes charge of making up a batch of one puree for the whole group. By the time you're finished, everyone will go home with a nice assortment of purees that can be used in dozens of recipes. It's quick, it's easy, and with your pals around, it won't feel like work at all.

Basic ingredients for party:
■ Friends and family (ideally four to sixteen people)
■ Food processors (one for about every three people; some will be washing and chopping while the other person is processing)

■ Fresh or frozen fruit/vegetables (each person chooses a puree and brings the ingredients)
■ Good music
■ Bottle of wine (optional)

Who does what:
■ Some people rinse produce
■ A few take charge of chopping
■ Others set up areas for each puree (green, purple, orange, white, white bean)
■ One person runs each food processor
■ Several people bag ¼-cup portions of each puree
■ Others label each bag with the name of the puree and the date it was prepared (always a good idea when you're storing something in the freezer)

Save the Cupcake

Dear Missy,

"I'm so grateful for your help with our school bake sale. Prior to your arrival on the scene, our elementary school had been compelled to virtually eliminate our traditional fund raising bake sale.

Parents and administrators just couldn't condone the sale of sugary baked goods to our kids, even if it would generate funds for projects that would otherwise benefit them. With their children's weight and health at stake, the bake sale could no longer be justified as an acceptable means to an end.

Then the Sneaky Chef came to town! We are now able to have the best of both worlds. Your recipes have saved our fund raiser without sacrificing the health of our kids.

Using bake sales as fundraisers is a vital element of any school system, and now the administration feels that we are being consistent with our wellness message. We are doing something to address the rising rates of obesity, and to counter the perpetuation of junk food.

Our thinking has changed, and spearheading it all was The Sneaky Chef Bake Sale. On the day of the sale, we presented ingredients for each recipe, showing whole grains, fruits and veggies, as well as the lower calories and fat — all in an attractive goody that the kids accepted as normal.

We had a puree party two weeks before the sale so that participating moms could have the purees on hand for when they were ready to bake. The party was incredibly productive and fun. We all left with a dozen baggies of purees to put into our assigned baked goods for the day of the sale.

Then we all went off and baked our goodies. Everyone told me that their recipes were incredibly easy to follow and turned out great.

When the actual day of the bake sale came, the kids were allowed to buy two items each. The proceeds went towards the Main Street School Library Makeover Fund, which is a fantastic cause. Everything looked totally 'normal' and kid friendly. All the parents were debating whether to let the kids in on the secret, but many of the kids already knew, since they had helped their parents make the items, and they were fine with it. Everything sold like hotcakes and was gobbled up in no time.

We played a game to try to guess what was in each item. The kids had a great time with this and loved the fact that they could have their cake and eat it, too! It was a huge success. I highly recommend a Sneaky Bake Sale to every PTSA around the country that wants to make their bake sales healthier. As you said, Missy, why ban the cupcake when you can just make it better?

Can you please give us some more bake sale recipes, like cakes, cookies, cupcakes, birthday cake, and especially quick fixes to packaged goods. Thank you for saving the cupcake!"

—Denise C., Irvington, NY (mother of 1)

My Family Has Remained Healthy

"My three-year-old son has missed maybe three days of school during the school year (as we all know, kids are always picking up the latest bug at school and bringing it home to the family). As I would listen to my friends talk about their whole family being sick and on antibiotics, I would always feel grateful and confident that my family has remained healthy and antibiotic-free due to healthy living and the Sneaky Chef's wonderful recipes and healthy food tips."

—Melissa C., Dallas, TX (mother of 1)

GLOSSARY OF SUPERFOODS:

Superfoods may not wear capes and masks or leap buildings in a single bound, but they do come to our rescue by protecting us against disease, just as a superhero would. These foods get their power from phytonutrients, antioxidants, and nutrient density, meaning they pack the most good-for-you punch with the fewest calories. You'll see that I use these foods in as many recipes as possible in this book, because I believe it's better to prevent health problems now than have to cure them later. My recipes will help you do just that—no cape needed.

Note: This glossary is meant for informational purposes only. If you have questions about your health, please consult your personal physician.

ALMONDS

Almonds are packed with nutrition. Don't worry about their fat content; they're the "good" heart-healthy kinds of fats like those in olives. Just a quarter cup of almonds boasts more protein than an egg, and they are rich in magnesium, potassium, calcium, iron, zinc, and vitamin E. They lower bad cholesterol and improve the good, and provide soluble fiber and antioxidants to strengthen the heart and fight disease. According to new research, the fiber in almonds may actually combat obesity and diabetes because it blocks the body's absorption of both fat and carbohydrates, which keeps your weight down and stabilizes your blood sugar. Since they are so satisfying, almonds often keep people from eating undesirable snacks. Anything enhanced by their flavor and texture will provide a sustained source of energy.

BANANAS

Most kids love them, making them a great staple to have on hand when they come home from school. When frozen, bananas are a nutrient-dense, sweet, non-fat, thickening base for quick homemade ice cream, smoothies, and milk shakes. Athletes have often applauded the energy delivered by bananas' high levels of potassium, as well as their complex carbohydrates for slow-burning energy. Since they neutralize stomach acid, they are easily digestible, even when children are feeling queasy. Bananas are so mild that they're often given to babies as their first solid food.

They also contain as much fiber as a slice of whole-grain bread and as much pectin as an apple, both of which maintain good intestinal health. They can replace the electrolytes lost from bouts with diarrhea and even build better bones by improving the body's ability to absorb calcium. What's more, they nourish the "good" bacteria in the colon (probiotics), the stuff that promotes wholesome digestion and strengthens the immune system. Bananas contain tryptophan, a calming nutrient, which makes them a perfect bedtime snack.

BLUEBERRIES

Blueberries have earned the name "super-fruit" and are number one in antioxidant power, according to researchers at the USDA. Their powerful flavonoids give them their high antioxdant properties, and they are one of the most nutrient-dense fruits, bursting with vitamins A and C, zinc, potassium, iron, calcium, magnesium, and fiber. Evidence confirms that blueberries help boost your immunity to everyday illnesses,

prevent disease in the future, and protect your heart. Now blueberries are being billed alongside cranberries for offering protection against urinary tract infections. They are also especially high in lutein, which keeps eyes healthy. Researchers have even found that diets rich in blueberries can significantly improve memory function and learning capacity. So toss a few blueberries into your kid's breakfast for an A+ meal.

BROCCOLI

This green veggie is one of the healthiest, most nutrient-dense foods on the planet. It is surprisingly high in protein and fiber, as well as calcium, so it strengthens growing bones and teeth. In just one half cup, you get two grams of fiber but 100 percent of the recommended daily value of vitamin C. It's an antioxidant that boosts immunity against everyday colds, the flu, heart disease, and all cancers.

CARROTS

Carrots might be a common vegetable, but they're not ordinary. Sometimes considered the "king of vegetables," carrots can boast that they are the richest source of carotenes and antioxidants in the vegetable realm. Some studies have shown that as little as one carrot a day can cut the risk of lung cancer in half. These orange beauties boost immunity, they're full of fiber (more than two grams in just one), and they strengthen the heart. Surprisingly, since we usually think of raw veggies as the healthiest, the nutrients in carrots are better absorbed when they are cooked, as they are in Orange Puree. Pureed carrots are also a helpful remedy to cut diarrhea short and speed the recovery time from illnesses.

"The whole family has benefited with fewer colds and less sickness and an overall happier disposition."

—Tina E., Australia (mum of six)

CAULIFLOWER

Packed with folate and fiber, cauliflower enhances immunity and fights disease. It also has a lot of vitamin C, and according to one large study, young children who have asthma experience significantly less wheezing if they eat a diet high in foods with vitamin C's antioxidant powers. It maintains healthy bones and skin and may protect against bruising. It strengthens the immune system, helping to prevent and fight colds, flu, and other illnesses.

CHERRIES

Cherries are referred to by some nutritionists as the "healing fruit." They're laden with vitamins A and C and have potassium, fiber, and antioxidants. Cherries are a good source of ellagic acid, a flavonoid that is a potent anticancer agent—it's also in blueberries. Studies have shown that cherries, especially tart ones, can reduce inflammation in the body, sometimes eliminating migraine headaches as effectively as aspirin or ibuprofen. They are also rich in the naturally occurring hormone melatonin, which slows aging and enhances sleep.

CHICKPEAS

These legumes are inexpensive, and given how satisfying they are, they're incredibly nutritious. They can lower cholesterol and blood pressure and prevent constipation. Like white beans, when they're added to high-carb/high-sugar foods, they stabilize blood sugar levels, providing slow-burning energy so that the kids are satisfied longer and have less of a heavy, groggy feeling after a meal. All beans are an excellent source of folate, magnesium, and iron, which are fantastic sources of energy, offer brain-boosting power, and give protection against heart disease and cancer. Chickpeas especially increase energy by replenishing iron stores, of particular importance for children who are at risk for iron deficiency.

GREEN PEAS

Green peas are a good source of fiber, vitamin C, and potassium. These little green marbles boost immunity, fight colds, and protect against heart disease and all types of cancer. They're high in vitamin K, which strengthens bones, and they have a lot of iron, so they inject high energy. Moms love them because they improve learning. Incredibly, one cup of green peas actually has more protein than a large egg.

LENTILS

Health Magazine has chosen lentils as one of the five healthiest foods on earth, and for good reason! This legume is a particularly good source of iron, which is especially important for growing children. Lentils are inexpensive, easy to prepare, and available all year long. Their high fiber content helps fight cholesterol, stabilize blood sugar, and provide slow and steady energy. Brown lentils still have their skin intact, so they have more fiber (32 percent) than red lentils (11 percent). In addition to their high fiber, lentils are loaded with protein, magnesium, and folate, three of the most important nutrients for heart health.

SPINACH

Spinach, with its rich green color, is a nutrient powerhouse. It contains twice as much iron as most other greens and is an excellent source of calcium, folic acid, and vitamins A and C. It even has a high beta-carotene content, which most people think only comes from orange vegetables. This offers great protection against asthma, all kinds of cancer, and heart disease. It's good for the eyes, growing bones, and brains.

STRAWBERRIES

These berries' dark red color spells great health benefits: potent antioxidants and a rich supply of vitamins. If your child eats eight strawberries, she'll have just ingested 140 percent of all the vitamin C she needs for the day. They're also a good source of folic acid, fiber, potassium, and disease-fighting phytochemicals. Make strawberry puree and you've created a concentrated dose of these immune-boosting nutrients as well as a sweet fat replacer in baked goods.

SWEET POTATOES AND YAMS

These spuds are rich in complex carbohydrates and fiber, B vitamins, and folate (good for the heart and brain), and they're packed with antioxidant vitamins C and E, carotenes, calcium, potassium, and iron. They're often called the "antidiabetic" food because they stabilize blood sugar levels, preventing "crash and burn." Sweet potatoes—filling, satisfying, and incredibly nutritious—are easy for parents to serve because they're a natural comfort food. An added bonus is that they're loaded with serotonin, so they boost moods, calming children and even helping them to sleep better. I use them because they add a subtle sweetness to sneaky recipes and, when combined with tomato sauce, cut acidity.

"I have only been doing this for a couple of weeks and my boys have had more healthy food lately than I think ever."

—Stephanie S., Manitoba, Canada (mother of 2)

WHEAT GERM

Wheat germ offers a great way to serve up nutrients; it's an excellent source of iron, protein, B vitamins, folic acid, and vitamin E. Now popular even outside the health food store, it is one of the best food sources of zinc, magnesium, manganese, and chromium. Its abundant levels of vitamin B nourish the whole nervous system, and it's believed to prevent fatigue and migraines.

WHITE BEANS

These include navy, butter, or cannellini. They're incredibly satisfying and nutritious, yet they cost pennies. They lower cholesterol and blood pressure and prevent constipation, and when added to high-carb/high-sugar foods, they stabilize blood sugar levels, providing steady, slow-burning energy so the kids will feel satisfied longer and undergo less "brain fog." All beans are an excellent source of folate as well as magnesium and iron, providing energy and power to boost the brain and protect against heart disease and cancer. White beans can increase energy by helping to replenish iron stores. This is especially important for children who suffer from iron deficiency. Combined with grains or rice, beans form a whole protein comparable to meat and dairy. Their creamy white color and very mild flavor make them an excellent sneaky ingredient in many recipes.

WHOLE-WHEAT FLOUR

This type of flour features many important nutrients that are stripped away when wheat is processed into white flour. Whole wheat is an excellent source of manganese, magnesium, and tryptophan. The fiber is wonderful because it regulates digestion, prevents constipation, and stabilizes blood sugar levels, making you feel satisfied longer. It also protects against insulin resistance, which can be a precursor to diabetes. Whole grains might be carbs, but they actually fight obesity. A Harvard Medical School study published in the November 2003 issue of the *American Journal of Clinical Nutrition* showed that women who consume a fiber-rich whole-grain diet weigh less than those who eat refined wheat products; those who ate the most dietary fiber from whole grains were 49 percent less likely to gain weight.

ZUCCHINI

This squash is great for dieters. It's low in calories, yet delicious. High in fiber, manganese, vitamin C, and potassium, it offers protection against asthma, certain cancers, high blood pressure, and heart disease. Other benefits include muscle strengthening, enhanced energy, clearer thinking, and a happier disposition. The delicate flavor and creamy white flesh make them an ideal choice for Sneaky Chefs because they blend into a myriad of dishes.

CHAPTER FOUR

Sneaky Chef
Every Day

Now that you've read about the Make-Aheads—the foundations for the Sneaky Chef recipes—you're ready to start cooking!

JUST A FEW NOTES BEFORE WE BEGIN.

1. The "Optional Extra Boost" at the bottom of many recipes is an ingredient that will add more nutrition, but we can't really classify it as disguised and invisible. Your kids will pick up on it, so make sure they like this flavor or texture before adding it. Otherwise, you run the risk of ruining the entire dish.

2. For each recipe, the sneaky ingredients are highlighted in gray.

3. All the purees can be frozen for up to three months and kept in the refrigerator for three days.

4. The truly skillful Sneaky Chef sneaks up on the family with these methods. That is to say, a Sneaky Chef uses only a small amount of the puree for the first

few times to acclimate their taste. You don't want to raise a red flag by overloading a dish with a new taste or texture. Instead, over time, gradually increase the amount of the booster, adding only as much as you can get away with.

5. For all the purees, it's perfectly all right to use frozen fruit and vegetables. The fact that they are frozen right after they're picked ensures that much of the vitamins and minerals has been locked in. I actually prefer frozen to fresh blueberries for just that reason. The "fresh" blueberries have sometimes been picked up to ten days before you buy them, whereas the frozen might have been picked the same day they were processed. (The only exception here is spinach—I strongly advise using only raw baby spinach, not frozen—because fresh young leaves will give you a much better taste that won't affect the overall flavor or texture of the recipe.)

6. I often refer to cooking spray oil in the recipes. Use an additive-free, natural olive oil or canola oil spray or mist, or make your own cooking spray by putting the healthy oil of your choice into a spray bottle.

6. You'll notice icons at the top of each recipe. They indicate nutrition highlights, and are a quick way to tell if the recipe fits into your goals:

 Whole Grains: includes a healthy amount of whole grains

 Veggie: vegetarian recipe (may include eggs and dairy, but no fish, poultry, or meat)

 Indulge: has a higher fat and/or sugar content

 Antioxidant Boost: contains a number of antioxidants

 Protein Boost: contains a good amount of protein

Low Carb: contains minimal carbohydrates; ideal for low-carb diets

 Low Sugar: contains no added sugar or sweeteners

 Omega-3s: contains a healthy amount of omega-3 fatty acids

 Healthy Fats: contains heart-healthy (monounsaturated) fats, like olive or nut oils, avocados, or nuts

Now you're ready to be the sneakiest chef in town, all for the greater good of your family. Virtually every email I have received has revealed that parents were absolutely giddy at the sight of their children eating the fruits, vegetables, and fiber that they wouldn't have touched before. And most kids are "in on it and love it" according to my readers! So let them help out in the kitchen.

Peanut Better Waffles

Some of us just can't get enough peanut butter (I'll take mine straight from a tablespoon, please). But since I can't make an entire recipe out of a spoon and a jar, these waffles are the next best thing.

MAKES 4 WAFFLES

6 tablespoons creamy peanut butter

2 large eggs

1 teaspoon pure vanilla extract

2 tablespoons pure maple syrup

½ cup Orange Puree (see Make-Ahead Recipe #2, p. 44)

2 teaspoons baking powder

¾ cup Flour Blend (see Make-Ahead Recipe #10, p. 56)

Preheat a waffle iron to medium-high and spray with oil.

In a large mixing bowl, whisk together the peanut butter, eggs, vanilla, maple syrup, and Orange Puree. In another large bowl, whisk together the baking powder and Flour Blend. Add the wet ingredients to the dry, stirring until just blended. The batter should be fairly thick and slightly lumpy.

Spoon ⅓ to ½ cup batter onto the center of the prepared waffle iron (the amount of batter needed will vary according to the size and type of the waffle iron you're using). Close the top and cook until the waffle is lightly

Sneaky Tip:

To make your morning breakfast quicker, you can make the batter for any of the sneaky pancake and waffle recipes the night before and leave it covered in the refrigerator overnight.

browned, crisp, and lifts easily off the grids, about 5 minutes. Repeat with the remaining batter, spraying the waffle iron with more oil if needed.

Serve immediately as the waffles come off the iron, or keep them warm on a plate, covered with aluminum foil. Serve drizzled with maple syrup or a dollop of fresh jam.

PER SERVING (1 WAFFLE, 114G): *Calories 304; Total Fat 15.6g; Fiber 4.4g; Total Carbohydrates 31.4g; Sugars 9.8g; Protein 13.0g; Sodium 347mg; Cholesterol 105mg; Calcium 216mg.* 25% less carbohydrates, 127% more fiber, and 40% more protein than traditional recipe.

Bacon, Egg, and Cheese Breakfast Sticks

I'm so jealous at the local deli when I hear the guys order "bacon, egg, and cheese on a buttered roll."
I can't believe anyone can actually eat that kind of food and still fit into the car. But it's a heck of a way
to go—yum! Here's my version, still decadent, but definitely an improvement over the original.

MAKES ABOUT 18 SERVINGS

1 cup old-fashioned rolled oats (not quick-cooking)

1 cup Flour Blend (see Make-Ahead Recipe #10, p. 56)

½ teaspoon salt

1 tablespoon unsalted butter

3 tablespoons packed brown sugar

¼ cup White Bean Puree (see Make-Ahead Recipe #9, p. 54)

2 large eggs

3 tablespoons buttermilk

1¼ cup shredded low-fat cheddar cheese

½ cup cooked bacon or ham, diced

Preheat oven to 375 degrees. Remove butter from refrigerator to let soften. Line an 11-by-7 inch baking pan with foil and spray the foil with oil.

In a large bowl, combine oats, Flour Blend, and salt. Set aside. In the bowl of an electric mixer, beat butter and sugar until creamy. Beat in White Bean Puree, eggs, and buttermilk. Mix in dry ingredients on low speed. Stir in one cup of the shredded cheese and ham or bacon. Pour entire mixture into prepared baking pan. Spread remaining quarter cup of cheese evenly over the top.

Bake for 22 to 24 minutes or until golden brown. Let cool on a metal rack.

Let cool before cutting into sticks (approximately 1-by-3-inch sticks). Store wrapped in refrigerator for up to 3 days, in the freezer up to 3 months.

PER SERVING (1 STICK, 39G): *Calories 105; Total Fat 4.3g; Fiber 1.3g; Total Carbohydrates 11.4g; Sugars 2.5g; Protein 5.4g; Sodium 161mg; Cholesterol 29mg; Calcium 49mg. 22% less calories, 49% less fat, 300% more fiber, 129% more potassium, and 67% more protein than traditional recipe.*

"Just like working out, it's become a habit to add purees to all our family's meals—and it feels great!"

—Denise G., Bala Cynwyd, PA (mother of 2)

Quick Fixes for Boxed Pancake Mix

You do it, I do it, we all do it. You know what I'm talking about. Dare I say out loud that we use boxed pancake mix instead of making pancakes from scratch!? C'mon, we live in the real world where convenience is a must. Here are several ways to add a nutritious homemade touch to your favorite boxed mix (I tested these with Aunt Jemima's Original):

Banana Pancakes:

1 large egg

¾ cup low-fat milk

1 tablespoon canola or vegetable oil

1 large banana, mashed

¼ cup **Orange Puree** (see Make-Ahead Recipe #2, p. 44)

1 cup boxed pancake mix

¼ cup wheat germ

In a large mixing bowl, whisk together the egg, milk, oil, banana, and Orange Puree. Add boxed pancake mix and wheat germ, mixing just until combined (don't overmix, leave small lumps). If the batter is too thick, add a little more milk.

PER SERVING (3 PANCAKES, 151G): *Calories 256; Total Fat 7.6g; Fiber 3.2g; Total Carbohydrates 39.2g; Sugars 7.3g; Protein 8.6g; Sodium 443mg; Cholesterol 61mg; Calcium 149mg.* 14% less fat, 57% more fiber, 46% more potassium, 12% less sodium, 27% more protein, and 17% less sugars than traditional recipe.

Chocolate Pancakes:

1 large egg

¾ cup low-fat milk

1 tablespoon canola or vegetable oil

½ cup **Purple Puree** (see Make-Ahead Recipe #1, p. 43)

1 cup boxed pancake mix

1 tablespoon unsweetened cocoa powder

¼ cup oat bran

¼ cup semi-sweet chocolate chips (optional)

PUREES

clockwise from back: Cherry Puree, Orange Puree, White Puree, White Bean Puree, Lentil Puree, Purple Puree, Green Puree

BACON, EGG & CHEESE BREAKFAST STICKS

Sneaky ingredients: Oats, white beans, wheat germ, whole wheat

QUICK FIXES FOR BOXED PANCAKE MIX

Sneaky ingredients (chocolate): Spinach, blueberries, oat bran

Sneaky ingredients (banana): Yams, carrots, wheat germ

PEANUT BETTER WAFFLES

Sneaky ingredients: Carrots, yams, wheat germ, whole wheat

SAMMY'S SCONES AND FUDGE SCONES

Sneaky ingredients: Oats, wheat germ, white beans, cherries, whole wheat

CRAVIN' COFFEE CAKE

Sneaky ingredients: White beans, wheat germ, whole wheat

LUNCH BOX MUFFINS (MAC 'N' CHEESE FLAVOR)

Sneaky ingredients: Carrots, yams

PASTA WITH BETTER BUTTER SAUCE

Sneaky ingredient: White beans

SNEAK-WICHES

Sneaky ingredients: Yams, carrots, strawberries

In a large mixing bowl, whisk together the egg, milk, oil, and Purple Puree. Add boxed pancake mix, cocoa powder, oat bran, and chocolate chips (if using), mixing just until combined (don't overmix, leave small lumps). If the batter is too thick, add a little more milk.

PER SERVING (3 PANCAKES, 137G): *Calories 226; Total Fat 7.5g; Fiber 3.1g; Total Carbohydrates 34.6g; Sugars 5.4g; Protein 8.2g; Sodium 442mg; Cholesterol 61mg; Calcium 157mg. 27% less calories, 29% less fat, 19% less cholesterol, 30% less carbs, 32% more potassium, 18% less sodium, and 72% less sugars than traditional recipe.*

Basic Whole Grain/Yogurt Pancakes:

1 large egg

¾ cup low-fat milk

1 tablespoon canola or vegetable oil

½ cup plain low-fat yogurt

1 cup boxed pancake mix

¼ cup wheat germ

In a large mixing bowl, whisk together the egg, milk, oil, and yogurt. Add boxed pancake mix and wheat germ, mixing just until combined (don't overmix, leave small lumps). If the batter is too thick, add a little more milk.

PER SERVING (3 PANCAKES, 132G): *Calories 235; Total Fat 8.5g; Fiber 1.8g; Total Carbohydrates 30.7g; Sugars 3.9g; Protein 9.1g; Sodium 447mg; Cholesterol 5mg; Calcium 179mg. 131% more fiber, 76% more potassium, 20% less sodium, and 25% more protein than traditional recipe.*

Brown Sugar and Cinnamon Pancakes:

1 large egg

¾ cup low-fat milk

1 tablespoon canola or vegetable oil

1 tablespoon packed brown sugar

½ teaspoon cinnamon

¼ cup oat bran

1 cup boxed pancake mix

In a large mixing bowl, whisk together the egg, milk, oil, brown sugar, and cinnamon. Add the oat bran and boxed pancake mix, mixing just until combined (don't overmix, leave small lumps). If the batter is too thick, add a little more milk.

PER SERVING (3 PANCAKES, 100G): *Calories 218; Total Fat 7.2g; Fiber 1.9g; Total Carbohydrates 33.0g; Sugars 5.9g; Protein 7.4g; Sodium 434mg; Cholesterol 61mg; Calcium 149mg. 22% less calories, 34% less fat, 22% less carbs, 27% more fiber, 34% more potassium, 157% more protein, and 73% less sugars than traditional recipe.*

French Toast Rollers

Turn French toast into a fun handheld food. Just flatten the bread, spread on your favorite fillings, and it becomes an event. My daughter Emily came up with this delicious idea and thought up all the variations. Don't be afraid to let your kids' imaginations run with this. Only you'll know about the secret purees.

MAKES 4 SERVINGS

2 large eggs

¼ cup low-fat milk

¼ teaspoon *each* cinnamon and salt

½ teaspoon pure vanilla extract

1 tablespoon honey

3 tablespoons Orange Puree
   (see Make-Ahead Recipe #2, p. 44)

4 slices bread (ideally whole wheat)

Powdered sugar, for dusting

Optional Fillings:

1 tablespoon peanut butter + 1 tablespoon Orange, Strawberry, or Cherry Puree (see Make-Ahead Recipe #2, p. 44, #6, p. 51, #7, or p. 52) (or other fruit spread)

1 mashed banana + 1 tablespoon Orange Puree (see Make-Ahead Recipe #2, p. 44)

1 tablespoon light cream cheese + 1 tablespoon Cherry Puree (see Make-Ahead Recipe #6, p. 52) (or other fruit spread)

Powdered sugar, for dusting

In a large shallow baking dish, whisk together the eggs, milk, cinnamon, salt, vanilla, honey, and Orange Puree. Set aside. Use a rolling pin to roll out each slice of bread on a cutting board until flattened. In a mixing bowl, mix the optional fillings. Spread about 2 tablespoons of the filling mixture on each flattened slice of bread, keeping about ¼ inch away from the edges. Roll up each slice of bread, pressing to seal the edges.

Dip each log roll in the egg mixture until saturated on all sides, then cook in a well-greased skillet over moderate heat, turning to brown each side. Remove from heat and lightly dust with powdered sugar before serving.

PER SERVING (1 ROLLER, NO FILLING, 80G):
Calories 133; Total Fat 3.8g; Fiber 2.2g; Total Carbohydrates 19.1g; Sugars 7.2g; Protein 6.5g; Sodium 338mg; Cholesterol 106mg; Calcium 56mg. 27% less calories, 45% less fat, 65% more potassium, 23% less carbs, 110% more fiber, and 17% more protein than traditional recipe.

"I have been battling my kids' eating peccadilloes for so long with such little luck that I nearly found myself physically shoving a salty, canned green bean into my daughter's face out of sheer exasperation, frustration, and concern over their eating habits. This book has changed our lives, literally. Dinner is fun and pleasant because we can talk instead of plead, yell, bargain, and lecture. Thanks for giving us health and me sanity!"

—*Meghan P., Prairie Village, KS (mother of 2)*

Inside-Out Snow Day French Toast

Dear Missy,

I wanted to share a fun recipe and tradition that my family enjoys every winter. When the weather forecasts predict serious snow, Rachel and Benjamin engage in a series of nighttime rituals in the hopes of bringing a snow day/day off from school. These rituals include wearing their pajamas inside out and backward. As a family we also prepare Inside-Out Snow Day French Toast before bed, and put it in the fridge to set overnight. When the kids get up at the crack of dawn to survey the snow and listen for school closing reports on the radio, we also pop the Inside-Out Snow Day French Toast in the oven so we can enjoy it as a celebratory breakfast in the event of a snow day, or as a treat to help take the edge off the disappointment of learning that it's going to be a regular old school day after all!

—Sharon H., Irvington, NY (mother of 2)

2 cups skim milk

2 large eggs

3 egg whites

2 tablespoons maple syrup

2 teaspoons pure vanilla extract

½ cup **White Bean Puree (see Make-Ahead Recipe #9, p. 54)**

1 teaspoon cinnamon

2 tablespoons butter, melted

¼ cup oat bran

6 slices whole-grain bread (cinnamon raisin works well), cut in half diagonally

Optional Garnish: whipped cream and maple syrup or cinnamon sugar

Preheat oven to 350 degrees and grease or spray a 2-quart (approximately 11 inches by 7 inches) glass baking dish.

In the prepared baking dish, whisk together all ingredients except the bread. Add the bread and toss to combine. Let sit for a few minutes (or cover with foil and refrigerate overnight) until the bread is soft and has absorbed most of the liquid.

Bake, uncovered, for 40 minutes, until golden brown

Serve warm, drizzled with maple syrup, and garnish with a squirt of whipped cream or a dusting of cinnamon sugar, if desired.

PER SERVING (154G): *Calories 198; Total Fat 6.2g; Fiber 3.3g; Total Carbohydrates 24.9g; Sugars 4.6g; Protein 11.2g; Sodium 223mg; Cholesterol 96mg; Calcium 143mg.*

Breakfast Banana Bread Pudding

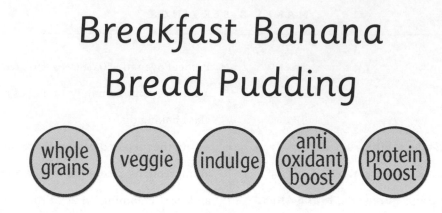

Inspired by Sharon's Inside-Out French Toast, I set out to create a similar banana bread pudding. My friends Amy and Rich had been to a cooking school and learned twelve new ways to make bread pudding, all of which were loaded with high-fat, artery-clogging, sinful ingredients. On a recent day off from school, the kids were playing hide-and-go-seek in the living room, while the grown-ups were playing the same game in the kitchen, but for a more serious purpose. We were trying to come up with a healthier version of bread pudding that we could eat for breakfast, with all the flavor and none of the guilt. Rich proclaimed this as satisfying as the vacation bread puddings!

MAKES 8 SERVINGS

1 cup low-fat milk

2 large eggs

2 egg whites

2 tablespoons maple syrup

1 teaspoon pure vanilla extract

¼ cup Orange Puree (see **Make-Ahead Recipe #2, p. 44**)

3 large bananas, mashed with the back of a fork (about 1½ cups)

½ teaspoon cinnamon

1 tablespoon butter, melted

6 slices whole-grain bread, cut or torn into 2" pieces

Preheat oven to 350 degrees and grease or spray a 2-quart (approximately 11 inches by 7 inches) glass baking dish.

In the prepared baking dish, whisk together all ingredients except the bread. Add the bread and toss to combine. Let sit for a few minutes (or cover with foil and refrigerate overnight) until the bread is soft and has absorbed most of the liquid.

Bake, covered, for 30 minutes, then uncover, sprinkle with a little more cinnamon, and continue baking for another 15 to 20 minutes, until top is golden brown and the pudding is firm in the center.

Serve warm, drizzled with maple syrup, if desired.

PER SERVING (277G): *Calories 329; Total Fat 8.1g; Fiber 6.6g; Total Carbohydrates 55.2g; Sugars 25.1g; Protein 12.4g; Sodium 343mg; Cholesterol 116mg; Calcium 139mg.* 35% less calories, 66% less fat, 36% less cholesterol, 15% less carbs, 330% more fiber, 87% more potassium, 20% more protein and 22% less sugars than traditional recipe.

Hot Cocoa Oatmeal

You know by now that there's no need to deprive anyone of childhood traditions in pursuit of a healthier lifestyle. Hot cocoa in front of the fire on a cold and snowy day is one of those delicious traditions that imprints warm memories deep into our psyches. But what if we could have the best of both worlds—rich chocolaty creaminess in a healthier package—and create a new tradition at the same time? Give this a try—it got my kids to eat oatmeal for the first time since they were babies.

MAKES 2 SERVINGS

½ cup old-fashioned rolled oats (not quick-cooking)

1½ cups low-fat milk

¼ cup Cherry Puree (see Make-Ahead Recipe #7, p. 52)

½ teaspoon cinnamon

¼ teaspoon salt

1 tablespoon unsweetened cocoa

1 tablespoon wheat germ

1 tablespoon honey or sugar

Mix all ingredients in pot and bring to a boil. Reduce to low, cover, and cook for 6 to 8 minutes until the oats are tender and the oatmeal has thickened.

PER SERVING (252G): *Calories 235; Total Fat 3.8g; Fiber 4.4g; Total Carbohydrates 32.4g; Sugars 25.1g; Protein 11.2g; Sodium 373mg; Cholesterol 9mg; Calcium 245mg.* 11% less carbs, 68% more protein than traditional recipe.

Grandma Betty's Cornflake and Cheese Pudding

I dedicate this recipe to my late Grandma Betty. As with many of the recipes passed down for generations, there's no way to replicate the exact taste of my wonderful Grandma's pudding (it was either the love—or some other secret ingredient she never wrote down—that made it taste different), but this is pretty darn close, even with all the extra healthful ingredients that I slipped in to give it a boost. I make this every Sunday and on rushed weekday mornings when I want to give the kids an instant hot breakfast.

MAKES 6 SERVINGS

2 cups whole-grain cereal flakes (like Wheaties or Total)

1½ cups low-fat cottage cheese (ideally "whipped")

2 large eggs

¼ cup White Bean Puree (see Make-Ahead Recipe #9, p. 54)

¼ teaspoon salt

⅓ cup sugar

2 teaspoons pure vanilla extract

Preheat oven to 375 degrees and grease or spray a loaf pan (approximately 9 inches by 5 inches) with oil.

Using a rolling pin, gently crush the cereal (in a sealed plastic bag) into coarsely crushed flakes. Alternatively, you can quickly pulse the cereal in a food processor. Set aside.

In a large mixing bowl, whisk together the cottage cheese, eggs, White Bean Puree, salt, sugar, and vanilla. Pour about ¾ of a cup of the crushed cereal on the bottom of the prepared loaf pan. Next, pour all of the cottage cheese mixture on top of the cereal, then top with the remaining crushed cereal. Spray the top with oil and bake for 45 minutes, uncovered. Serve with drizzle of maple syrup.

PER SERVING (99G): *Calories 179; Total Fat 3.1g; Fiber 1.9g; Total Carbohydrates 25.3g; Sugars 12.9g; Protein 12.1g; Sodium 420mg; Cholesterol 75mg; Calcium 61mg.* 840% more fiber, and 220% more protein than traditional recipe.

Monkey Pancakes

I'm beginning to think all kids' foods should be served in the form of a pancake, a meatball, or an ice cream cone! Put on Jack Johnson's "banana pancakes" song and make these with your child. Prepare a couple of batches on Sunday morning and freeze them in a plastic bag—presto, instant toaster pancakes!

MAKES ABOUT 14 PANCAKES (APPROXIMATELY 3" ROUND)

2 large bananas, mashed with the back of a fork (about 1 cup)

¼ cup **Orange Puree (see Make-Ahead Recipe #2, p. 44)**

1 large egg

1 tablespoon maple syrup

¼ cup low-fat milk

½ cup **Flour Blend (see Make-Ahead Recipe #10, p. 56)**

1 teaspoon baking powder

¼ teaspoon salt

Preheat griddle to medium-high and spray with oil.

In a medium bowl, whisk together the bananas, Orange Puree, egg, maple syrup, and milk. In another large bowl, whisk the Flour Blend, baking powder, and salt. Add the wet ingredients to the dry ones until just blended. If the batter is too thick, add a touch more milk.

Test the pan by tossing in a few drops of water; it will sizzle when it's hot enough. The skillet will grow hotter over time, so turn down the heat if the pan starts to smoke.

Drop medium-size ladles of batter onto the skillet in batches. When bubbles begin to set around the edges and the skillet side of each pancake is golden (peek underneath), gently flip them over. Continue to cook 2 to 3 minutes or until the pancake is fully set.

Serve stacked high, drizzled with a little warm maple syrup.

PER SERVING (1 PANCAKE, 38G): *Calories 46; Total Fat 0.6g; Fiber 1.0g; Total Carbohydrates 9.2g; Sugars 3.7g; Protein 1.5g; Sodium 77mg; Cholesterol 15mg; Calcium 37mg.* 32% less calories, 73% less fat, 39% less sodium, 58% more potassium, 11% less carbs, and 94% more fiber than traditional recipe.

Peanut Butter Monkey Pancake Variation:

Follow the instructions for Monkey Pancakes, but use only 1 large banana and add ¼ cup smooth peanut butter into the batter.

He Proudly Eats What He Makes!

I started off being very sneaky in the kitchen, not letting anyone know what I was doing. Once everyone ate and seemed to enjoy their food, I would tell them what I'd done. Now my four-year-old son and I make the sneaky recipes together and he very proudly eats what he makes. He's aware of what he's eating, and he thinks it's hilarious that we are being "sneaky" even though he knows what's going on. It's awesome! We'd love some more recipes like pancakes that we can make together.

—Lisa B., Lilburn, GA (mother of 2)

Sneaky Chef Note:

The following story was shared by a wonderful family friend whose father offers a tiny piece of dark chocolate as a "wake-up treat." Although not the healthiest idea, it represents a sweet family tradition that can be adapted in any number of healthy ways. Whether it's a bite of a fresh ripe peach or a tiny bite of chocolate to wake you up, it's wonderful to create a tradition in your family.

Something Fun and Different—Wake-Up Chocolate!

by Daphne K., Irvington, NY (age 11)

My brothers and sisters and I used to never get up in the morning. Our parents tried hard with alarms and yelling and putting us to sleep earlier. Nothing worked. Once I even had an alarm that sounded like a rooster that went "cock-a-doodle-doo." This was okay when I was little, but when I started first grade, I had to get up earlier. So my dad tried a trick from when he was little back in Greece. He started giving us what he calls "wake-up chocolate" to help us get up. The results are amazing!

So he usually does it on weekdays because no one in their right mind wakes up on weekdays like a normal human being. My dad wakes up very early and he gets all dressed for work (he's a pediatrician) and you hear his big shoes on the floor of the hall-way. You get ready, relax your muscles trying to look asleep. Then you hear him tiptoe into your room and you turn your head toward the noise of the crinkle of a tinfoil wrapper and the snap as he breaks a little

piece of chocolate off. You sense the chocolate coming near you—you smell it as it's closer to your face, then the chocolate touches your lips and you open your mouth and then you let it just melt. You never chew it; that's against the rules—you let it melt little by little and you feel your strength building (then you remember the homework you forgot to do!).

It makes you feel special. I mean, who gets chocolate in the morning? My dad said when he was little his mom used to do the same thing, and he does it exactly the same way. On my dad's birthday last year, my little brothers and sister and I got up early and did the same thing to him . . . we gave him breakfast chocolate! He freaked out!

People can try this with other sweet things—but it has to be something you love to eat. It has to be something good that'll wake you up. If it's last night's broccoli, it won't work! They'll run away from you!

Strawberry-Vanilla Breakfast Cookies

Breakfast cookies were one of the most popular items in my first book. Moms often enjoyed them for themselves and asked me to make more variations and give them nutritional analysis. Here are two new flavors, each offering fewer calories and sugar than most packaged granolas. Keep a batch in your freezer, grab and go, or even break them up and serve as "cold cereal" in a bowl with milk.

MAKES ABOUT 4 DOZEN COOKIES

6 tablespoons butter

1 cup Flour Blend (*see Make-Ahead Recipe #10, p. 56*)

1 teaspoon baking soda

½ teaspoon salt

3 cups old-fashioned rolled oats (not quick-cooking)

2 large eggs

2 teaspoons pure vanilla extract

1 cup Strawberry Puree (*see Make-Ahead Recipe #6, p. 61*)

½ cup brown sugar, packed

¼ cup strawberry jam (optional)

Preheat oven to 350 degrees. Line a baking sheet with parchment paper.

Melt butter in a microwave-safe glass or ceramic bowl in microwave on high for one minute (cover with a wet paper towel).

In a large bowl, whisk together Flour Blend, baking soda, salt, and oats. Set aside.

In another large bowl, whisk together eggs, vanilla, Strawberry Puree, sugar, and the melted butter.

Stir the dry ingredients into the wet ingredients until the dry ingredients are just moistened. Drop single tablespoonfuls onto the baking sheet, leaving about an inch between cookies. Make a small indent with your finger on each cookie and fill with about ½ teaspoon of jam, if using.

Bake for 25 to 28 minutes or until golden brown. Let cool on a metal rack.

Store cookies in airtight container for up to 3 days, or freeze them in a plastic bag for up to 3 months.

PER SERVING (1 COOKIE, 22G): *Calories 50; Total Fat 1.8g; Fiber .9g; Total Carbohydrates 7.5g; Sugars 2.5g; Protein 1.4g; Sodium 57mg; Cholesterol 11mg; Calcium 8mg.* 59% less calories, 57% less carbs, 69% less fat, and 77% less sugars than traditional recipe.

Cinnamon-Raisin Breakfast Cookies

MAKES ABOUT 4 DOZEN COOKIES

1½ cups Flour Blend
(see Make-Ahead
Recipe #10, p. 56)

1 teaspoon baking soda

½ teaspoon salt

1 teaspoon cinnamon

3 cups old-fashioned
rolled oats (not quick-
cooking)

2 large eggs

1 cup White Bean Puree
(see Make-Ahead
Recipe #9, p. 54)

½ cup packed brown sugar

4 tablespoons butter,
melted

1 cup raisins

Preheat oven to 350 degrees. Line a baking sheet with parchment paper.

In a large bowl, whisk together Flour Blend, baking soda, salt, cinnamon, and oats. Set aside.

In another large bowl, whisk together eggs, White Bean Puree, sugar, and melted butter.

Stir the dry ingredients into the wet ingredients until the dry ingredients are just moistened. Stir in raisins, then drop single tablespoonfuls onto the baking sheet, leaving about an inch between cookies.

Bake for 20 to 25 minutes or until golden brown. Let cool on a metal rack.

Serve with a glass of cold milk.

Store cookies in airtight container for up to 3 days, or freeze them in a plastic bag for up to 3 months.

PER SERVING (1 COOKIE, 21G): *Calories 64; Total Fat 1.5g; Fiber 1.2g; Total Carbohydrates 11.1g; Sugars 3.6g; Protein 2.1g; Sodium 55mg; Cholesterol 10mg.* 45% less calories, 33% less carbs, 73% less fat, 66% less sugars, and 49% more fiber than traditional recipe.

Sammy's Scones

I named these scones for my youngest daughter Sammy, who helped me perfect this recipe. I think the dictionary definition of a scone is something like a cross between a muffin and a cookie. These make for a lovely tea party with the girls after school, and they freeze well so they're ready to warm anytime with a dollop of sweet jam.

MAKES 8 SCONES

1½ cups Flour Blend (see Make-Ahead Recipe #10, p. 56)

½ cup old-fashioned rolled oats (not quick-cooking)

½ teaspoon *each* salt and baking soda

2 teaspoons baking powder

5 tablespoons cold unsalted butter, cut into bits

¼ cup White Bean Puree (see Make-Ahead Recipe #9, p. 54)

Powdered sugar, for dusting

¼ cup low-fat ricotta cheese

¼ cup low-fat buttermilk

1 large egg plus 1 egg for egg wash

2 teaspoons pure vanilla extract

¼ cup sugar

1 cup dried cherries or blueberries

½ cup semi sweet chocolate chips (optional)

Preheat oven to 400 degrees; grease (or spray oil in) the center area of a baking sheet.

In a large bowl, whisk together the Flour Blend, oats, salt, baking soda, and baking powder. Using your fingertips, work the butter into the dry mixture evenly, forming little pea-sized clumps.

In another bowl, whisk together the White Bean Puree, ricotta, buttermilk, 1 egg, vanilla, and sugar. Add the dry ingredients to the wet and mix just enough to moisten the dry ingredients. Stir in cherries or berries, and chocolate chips, if using.

Place dough on prepared baking sheet and form a large circle (about 8" in diameter). Cut into 8 wedges using a serrated knife. In a small bowl, beat the remaining egg with a teaspoon of water. Brush the tops of each wedge with egg wash and dust with sugar.

Bake for 14 to 16 minutes or until the edges are lightly browned and a toothpick inserted in the center comes out clean.

PER SERVING (1 SCONE, 103G): *Calories 310; Total Fat 10.8g; Fiber 8.2g; Total Carbohydrates 61g; Sugars 16g; Protein 8.5g; Sodium 353mg; Cholesterol 76mg; Calcium 134mg.* 11% less fat, 33% more protein, and 540% more fiber than traditional recipe.

Fudge Scones

MAKES 8 SCONES

1½ cups Flour Blend (see Make-Ahead Recipe #10, p. 56)

½ cup old-fashioned rolled oats (not quick-cooking)

½ teaspoon *each* salt and baking soda

2 teaspoons baking powder

¼ cup unsweetened cocoa powder

5 tablespoons cold butter, cut into pieces

¼ cup Purple Puree (see Make-Ahead Recipe #1, p. 43)

¼ cup low-fat ricotta cheese

¼ cup low-fat buttermilk

1 large egg plus 1 egg for egg wash

½ cup sugar

2 teaspoons pure vanilla extract

½ cup semisweet chocolate chips

Preheat oven to 400 degrees; grease (or spray oil in) the center area of a baking sheet.

In a large bowl, whisk together the Flour Blend, oats, salt, baking soda, baking powder, and cocoa. Using your fingertips, work the butter into the dry mixture evenly, forming little pea-sized clumps.

In another bowl, whisk together the Purple Puree, ricotta, buttermilk, 1 egg, sugar, and vanilla. Add the dry ingredients to the wet and mix just enough to moisten the dry ingredients. Stir in the chocolate chips.

Place dough on prepared baking sheet and form a large circle (about 8" in diameter). Cut into 8 wedges using a serrated knife. In a small bowl, beat the remaining egg with a teaspoon of water. Brush the tops of each wedge with egg wash and dust with sugar.

Bake for 14 to 16 minutes until the edges are lightly browned and a toothpick inserted in the center comes out clean.

PER SERVING (1 SCONE, 102G): *Calories 310; Total Fat 14.3g; Fiber 4.3g; Total Carbohydrates 41.3g; Sugars 19.7g; Protein 8.2g; Sodium 403mg; Cholesterol 76mg; Calcium 138mg.* 14% less calories, 31% less fat, 104% more fiber, 91% more potassium, and 80% more protein than traditional recipe.

Mom's Barley Breakfast Bars

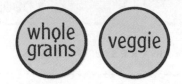

This recipe was generously donated by Karen G. Many moms told me they enjoyed the breakfast cookies partly because they found them convenient, satisfying, and filling. Many wanted more, so here is another quick breakfast especially for busy moms. I always make a few batches at a time and freeze them in bars. Aside from being convenient and low-fat, as well as packed with whole grains and fiber, they happen to be the right grains for breakfast. A recent Swedish study found that eating whole-grain barley or rye can help regulate blood sugar for the rest of day, which may aid in weight management.

MAKES 2 DOZEN BARS

2 large eggs

4 egg whites

1 teaspoon salt

½ cup canola or almond oil

¼ cup honey

1 cup old-fashioned rolled oats
(not quick-cooking)

1 cup cooked barley

2 teaspoons cinnamon

1 cup Flour Blend (see Make-Ahead
Recipe #10, p. 56)

Optional Extra Boost: ½ cup each chopped
walnuts and/or raisins

Sneaky Tip:

**Look for eggs with
added Omega-3's.**

Preheat oven to 350 degrees. Line a 13-by-9 inch baking pan completely with foil and butter the foil (or spray with oil)

In a large mixing bowl, whisk together the eggs, egg whites, salt, oil, and honey. Stir in the oats, barley, cinnamon, Flour Blend, and walnuts and/or raisins, if using. Mix well, then pour into the prepared baking pan. Press down with palm of hand, evenly distributing the mixture into the corners of the dish, and bake for 30 to 35 minutes. Check occasionally to prevent burning.

Remove from the oven and, using the foil to help you, lift the giant bar out of the pan. Place on a flat surface and, while still warm, cut into small bars, approximately 1" x 3".

Store in an airtight container for up to a week, or freeze in plastic bags.

PER SERVING (1 BAR, 33G): *Calories 99; Total Fat 5.4g; Fiber 1.2g; Total Carbohydrates 10.6g; Sugars 3.1g; Protein 2.6g; Sodium 112mg; Cholesterol 17mg; Calcium 9mg. 75% more potassium, 49% more fiber, and 51% more protein than traditional recipe.*

"I really love your book. Any plans for another Sneaky Chef book with the nutritional info included? Your recipes look so delicious and nutritious . . . it would be nice to see how nutritious they really are."

—*Lee Ann J., Toronto, Canada*

LUNCH RECIPES

*"My 4-year-old loves pasta with butter. Seems impossible
to sneak anything in there. Can you please help?"*

—Nicole S., Manhasset, NY (mother of 2)

Pasta with Better Butter Sauce

Plain pasta with butter presents the ultimate challenge for Sneaky Chefs, yet it's the universal favorite among the "no tomato sauce" set. You can sneak in some White Bean Puree as long as you use grated Parmesan cheese as a decoy on top. Who doesn't love cheese on their pasta? Aside from the fiber and added vitamins from the beans, the combination of beans and pasta creates a "complete protein" out of this normally no-protein, high-carb meal.

MAKE 4 SERVINGS

1 tablespoon butter

1 teaspoon olive oil

½ cup chicken broth, ideally low-sodium

¼ cup White Bean Puree (see Make-Ahead
  Recipe #9, p. 54)

4 cups cooked small pasta (such as elbows,
  ideally whole wheat)

3 to 4 tablespoons Parmesan cheese (optional)

In a saucepan, melt the butter with the olive oil, chicken broth, and White Bean Puree over low heat. Add the pasta and toss to evenly coat all pieces. Serve with Parmesan cheese, if desired.

PER SERVING (198G): *Calories 244; Total Fat 5.0g; Fiber 5.2g; Total Carbohydrates 43.3g; Sugars 1.2g; Protein 10.0g; Sodium 34mg; Cholesterol 7mg; Calcium 42mg. 66% less calories, 40% less fat, 54% less cholesterol, 67% less carbs, 90% less sodium, and 64% less sugars than traditional recipe.*

*"What recipes would you recommend for school lunch boxes?
I need something that does not need to be heated up and does not
contain nuts. My kiddos are getting tired of sandwiches!"*

—Shelley N., Richardson, TX (mother of 2)

Lunch Box Biscuits

*A great alternative to sandwiches, this lunch box biscuit offers protein, veggies, and whole grains
in a fun, portable package. Drop biscuits are easier to make than biscuits that require kneading and
rolling; plus you can get more of the healthy purees into them. Make a few batches once a month
and store them in the freezer; take one out to thaw in the refrigerator overnight and pop into your
kids' lunch boxes.*

MAKES 14 BISCUITS

2 cups Flour Blend (see Make-Ahead
　Recipe #10, p. 56)

1 tablespoon baking powder

1 teaspoon salt

½ teaspoon baking soda

4 tablespoons cold, unsalted butter,
　cut into small pieces

¼ cup plain yogurt

¾ cup White Puree (see Make-Ahead
　Recipe #4, p. 48)

¼ cup low-fat buttermilk

1 cup shredded low-fat cheddar cheese
　plus extra ½ cup for tops of biscuits

Optional "Mix-Ins":

Cheesier Biscuits:

½ cup shredded low-fat cheese

Ham and Cheese Biscuits:

½ cup shredded low-fat cheese and 2 cups diced, cooked ham (about 8 ounces)

Turkey and Cheese Biscuits:

½ cup shredded low-fat cheese and 2 cups diced, cooked turkey breast (about 8 ounces)

Bacon and Cheese Biscuits:

½ cup shredded low-fat cheese and 1 cup diced, cooked bacon

Preheat oven to 450 degrees; line a baking sheet with parchment paper (or spray with oil).

In a large bowl, whisk together the Flour Blend, baking powder, salt, and baking soda. Using your fingertips, work the butter into the dry mixture evenly, forming little pea-sized clumps.

In another bowl, whisk together the yogurt, White Puree, buttermilk, and 1 cup of shredded cheese. Add the dry ingredients to the wet and mix just enough to moisten the dry ingredients.

Stir in the "mix-ins" of choice.

Drop ¼-cup amounts of dough on prepared baking sheet. Top each biscuit with about a tablespoon of shredded cheese, and then spray the tops with oil.

Bake for 18 to 20 minutes or until the edges are lightly browned.

PER SERVING (1 PLAIN BISCUIT, 55G): *Calories 118; Total Fat 5.0g; Fiber 1.8g; Total Carbohydrates 12.9g; Sugars 0.8g; Protein 6.1g; Sodium 373mg; Cholesterol 12mg.* 26% less calories, 42% less fat, 69% less cholesterol, 313% more fiber, 131% more potassium, and 57% less sugars than traditional recipe.

Sneaky "Bonbons"

A "bonbon" is a European candy with a soft center. The connotation is that it's decadent, European, and reserved for the rich and famous! In reality, this is one of the healthiest recipes in this book. Kids may think they're having a delicious treat, but these bonbons are actually loaded with veggies, whole grains, and peanut butter, which has benefits like vitamin E, folate, and fiber! The sugar on the outside is your decoy—but it amounts to very little, and if it gets the kids to eat these healthy gems, then go for it. Make a few batches, freeze them, then toss a few in the lunch box frozen. They'll defrost perfectly by snack or lunch time at school.

MAKES 2 DOZEN PIECES

Toppings: 3 tablespoons sugar, cinnamon sugar, or sprinkles

½ cup **Orange Puree (see Make-Ahead Recipe #2, p. 44)**

¼ cup creamy peanut butter

¼ cup wheat germ

½ cup old-fashioned rolled oats (not quick-cooking)

½ cup semisweet chocolate chips, optional

Pour garnish toppings onto parchment paper or a plate and set aside. In a mixing bowl, combine Orange Puree and peanut butter. Mix in wheat germ, oats, and chocolate chips, if using, then pinch off heaping teaspoon-sized amounts of batter and roll into a ball with your hands. Roll balls in topping to coat completely. Wrap each ball individually in plastic wrap and freeze for up to 3 months.

PER SERVING (1 BONBON, 12G): *Calories 35; Total Fat 1.6g; Fiber 0.6g; Total Carbohydrates 4.5g; Sugars 2.1g; Protein 1.3g; Sodium 15mg; Cholesterol 0mg.* 50% less calories, 60% less fat, 100% less cholesterol, and 20% more fiber.

Chocolate-Dipped Bonbon Variation:

Make bonbons according to above instructions, omitting the topping and chocolate chips. Allow bonbons to harden in the freezer. Meanwhile, melt 1 cup of chocolate chips in a double boiler, a metal bowl over simmering water, or a microwave, checking every 15 seconds. Roll bonbons in melted chocolate. Let the excess chocolate drip off, then place the bonbons on parchment paper. Dust with sprinkles, if using, and allow to harden, refrigerating to cool more quickly if desired.

Elmwood's Tuna Elbows

whole grains | protein boost | omega 3s

My daughter Sammy came home every day from Elmwood Day Camp begging for the camp's delicious "Tuna Elbows," so together she and I recreated them at home. Use light tuna, which has less mercury, and use sardines to make it even lighter (green peas optional).

MAKES ABOUT 4 SERVINGS

3 tablespoons low-fat mayonnaise

¼ cup **White Bean Puree (see Make-Ahead Recipe #9, p. 54)**

¼ teaspoon salt

2 tablespoons oat bran

1 tablespoon freshly squeezed lemon juice

1 can (6 ounces) chunk light tuna, packed in water, drained

1 can (3 to 4 ounces) skinless and boneless sardines, packed in water, drained

½ pound (2 cups) macaroni elbows, cooked (ideally whole wheat)

Freshly ground pepper, to taste

Optional Extra Boost: ½ cup green peas and/or chopped celery

In a large serving bowl, whisk together mayonnaise, White Bean Puree, salt, oat bran, and lemon juice. Add in tuna and sardines and mix well with a fork. Add macaroni and any optional extra boosts and toss. Serve cold.

PER SERVING (159G): *Calories 365; Total Fat 4.0g; Fiber 3.6g; Total Carbohydrates 53.3g; Sugars 1.8g; Protein 25.1g; Sodium 352mg; Cholesterol 49mg; Calcium 118mg. 66% less fat, 25% less sodium, 40% more potassium, 51% more fiber, 42% less sugars, and 103% more protein than traditional recipe.*

Grilled Cheese and Tomato Soup

The best of all wintery meals, this new recipe matches tummy-warming tomato soup with mini grilled cheese croutons for great crunch and flavor. Who can tell while crunching and sipping that at least five superfoods are in this cold-weather lunch?

MAKES 6 SERVINGS

1 tablespoon olive oil

1 onion, finely diced or pureed

1 can (28 ounces) crushed tomatoes

2 cups vegetable or chicken broth, ideally low-sodium

½ cup White Bean Puree (see Make-Ahead Recipe #9, p. 54)

1 cup White or Orange Puree (see Make-Ahead Recipe #4, p. 48 or #2, p. 44)

1 cup fat-free evaporated milk

4 ounces American cheese

Salt and freshly ground pepper, to taste

Note: see Quick Fixes for Canned Soups, page 121, for shortcuts

For the croutons:

3 slices whole-grain bread, cut into 2 small circles each

2 ounces American cheese

Heat oil over medium heat in a soup pot or Dutch oven. Cook the onions until they are slightly translucent, and then add the crushed tomatoes, broth, White Bean Puree, and White or Orange Puree. Bring to a simmer for 10 to 15 minutes, stirring occasionally. Add the evaporated milk and cheese and simmer for another few minutes until all the cheese has melted.

Season with salt and pepper to taste.

Remove soup from heat and ladle into individual bowls. Top each bowl with a cheese crouton.

To make the croutons:

Divide the cheese equally on top of each bread round and toast lightly until the cheese is melted and bubbly. Lay croutons on top of the soup.

> **PER SERVING (1 BOWL, 383G):** *Calories 300; Total Fat 10.8g; Fiber 5.9g; Total Carbohydrates 37.8g; Sugars 13.1g; Protein 16.0g; Sodium 733mg; Cholesterol 19mg; Calcium 355mg. 32% less calories, 52% less sodium, 45% more potassium, 38% less carbs, and 32% less fat than traditional recipe.*

"My kids have unknowingly eaten more vegetables in the last few weeks than they have in their entire lives"

—Marion W., Shepherdstown, WV (mother of 2)

Sneak It!

Dear Sneaky Chef,

I've been making the usual school lunches for my kids for years now, and I would love to have some more variety to add to the mix. My kids are muffin maniacs, so anything in muffin form would be awesome!

I've been sneaking your purees onto their sandwiches for a while now and have only received rave reviews. The orange puree actually makes ketchup and marinara sauces sweeter because of the yams, so my kids love it and the best part is they don't know that it's actually good for them. Getting them to eat a "yicky" orange vegetable before this was a truly difficult experience. I'm just about ready to try making them an entirely orange puree sandwich and I'm confident they'll love it. I need to think up a name though... The white puree of cauliflower and zucchini hides well in the layer of mayo that the kids love on their sandwiches.

My family's always loved breakfast muffins and I'm sure they'll go for a lunch box muffin if I offer it. But I need it to pack a little protein since empty carbs won't last them and then I'll have a hungry mob on my hands by the time they get home. It's really in my own best interest to pack their lunches with hearty fare so they're not starving when they walk in the door. I swear they must burn up half their calories everyday just fidgeting in their chairs while watching TV! (If only I could do that...) Sorry for running on, but got any more good muffin recipes?

—Denise G., Bala Cynwyd, PA (mother of 2)

Portable Pizza Muffins

These are great in the lunch box, especially for kids who are bored with sandwiches. They get three top-notch veggies, three whole grains, calcium, and protein all in a portable package of a muffin. Kids love anything called "pizza." They are also a great after-school snack.

MAKES 8 MUFFINS

1 cup Flour Blend (see Make-Ahead Recipe #10, p. 56)

2 teaspoons baking powder

½ teaspoon baking soda

½ teaspoon *each* salt and dried oregano and/or basil

2 large eggs

2 tablespoons brown sugar, packed

3 tablespoons canola or vegetable oil

¼ cup tomato paste plus 3 tablespoons tomato paste (for the tops)

½ cup Orange Puree (see Make-Ahead Recipe #2, p. 44)

1 cup grated Parmesan cheese

Optional Extra Boost: 1 cup chopped mushrooms, onions, and/or olives

Preheat oven to 350 degrees and grease 8 cups in a 12-muffin pan or line 8 cups with paper muffin cups.

In a large bowl, whisk together the Flour Blend, baking powder, baking soda, salt, and oregano (and/or basil). In another large bowl, whisk together the eggs, brown sugar, canola or vegetable oil, ¼ cup of the tomato paste, Orange Puree, and ½ cup of the grated Parmesan cheese until well combined. Fold the wet ingredients into the dry and mix until the flour is just moistened. Stir in optional extras, if using. Don't overmix.

Divide the batter evenly among the 8 muffin cups. Top each muffin with a dollop (teaspoon) of tomato paste and about 1 tablespoon of Parmesan.

Bake 25 to 30 minutes, until a toothpick inserted in the center comes out clean. Turn the muffins out of the tins to cool, or serve warm.

PER SERVING (1 MUFFIN, 82G): *Calories 182; Total Fat 9.0g; Fiber 2.7g; Total Carbohydrates 19.6g; Sugars 6.3g; Protein 7.2g; Sodium 558mg; Cholesterol 58mg; Calcium 181mg.* 23% less calories, 30% less fat, 172% more potassium, and 185% more fiber than traditional recipe.

Quick Fixes for Canned Soup

veggie · anti oxidant boost · protein boost · low carb · low sugar

Our busy lives don't always allow us the luxury of preparing a soup from scratch. With your sneaky purees on hand, a healthy lunch or dinner is made in an instant by simply mixing in some purees with your family's favorite canned, boxed, or even store-bought "fresh" soups. The purees not only add a homemade feel to a packaged food, but they significantly enhance the flavor and nutrition.

Use the following rough guidelines to add to prepared soups; start with about 2 tablespoons of puree per serving of soup (add ¼ cup of puree to a can of soup that serves 2):

PUREE:	MIX INTO:
White Bean Puree	Broth-based soups
Orange or White Puree	Tomato-based soups
Orange or White Puree	Bean-based soups
White Bean or White Puree	Creamy soups
Green Puree (mix Green Puree with equal parts tomato paste to turn brown first, then add to beefy soup)	Beefy soups
Orange, White Bean, or White Puree	Beefy soups

Sneak-wiches

whole grains | veggie | anti oxidant boost | protein boost | low sugar

By now you know what a fan I am of taking time to make things ahead so they are ready to grab when I'm in a rush. "Sneak-wiches" are a good example of this method. Much like the packaged versions in the grocery store, this is a homemade, healthier version of the convenient made-ahead sandwich that you keep in the freezer. The key is to remove the crusts of the bread and crimp together the edges to "seal" the sandwich together. I suggest making several sandwiches at a time and freezing each individually in a plastic bag. There are several filling options below.

MAKES 1 SANDWICH

2 slices sandwich bread, ideally whole grain

Choose fillings below

Filling options: mix puree with other ingredient, then spread on each side of bread

—1 tablespoon *each* Orange Puree and Tomato Sauce plus 1–2 tablespoons cheese
—1 tablespoon *each* Orange Puree (or White Bean Puree) and peanut butter, plus jam, if desired
—1 tablespoon *each* Cherry or Strawberry Puree and light cream cheese

—1 tablespoon *each* Orange Puree and shredded cheese plus 1–2 slices ham
—1 tablespoon light cream cheese mixed with mashed sardines (and/or tuna)
—1 tablespoon *each* Green Puree and mashed avocado, plus cucumber slices if desired

Trim crust off bread. Use a rolling pin to roll out each slice of bread on a cutting board until flattened (alternatively, use the palm of your hand to flatten the bread). In a small bowl, mix the filling ingredients. Spread about a tablespoon of the fillings on each flattened slice of bread, keeping about ¼ inch away from the edges. Crimp the edges together with your fingers, then put sandwich in a plastic bag and freeze until ready to eat. Put in lunch box frozen, and it will defrost by lunch time.

"I have even used the White Bean Puree on turkey and cheese sandwiches and they love it."

—Al P., Birmingham, AL (stay-at-home dad of triplets)

Sneak 'n' Slice Pizza Bites

whole grains · veggie · indulge · anti oxidant boost · low sugar

With all the fun and flavor of traditional pizza, this rolled-up version is easy to handle and stores great in the freezer for a handy snack or light lunch. Slice off a few pieces and toast them up for an instant sandwich alternative or party finger food.

MAKES 1 SERVING

1 to 2 tablespoons pizza sauce

1 tablespoon Orange or White Puree (see Make-Ahead Recipe #2, p. 44 or #4, p. 48)

One (8- to 10-inch) flour tortilla, ideally whole wheat

2 to 3 tablespoons shredded low-fat mozzarella cheese

In a mixing bowl, stir together pizza sauce and Orange or White Puree. Spread the sauce mixture onto the tortilla (stay about ½ inch away from the edge). Sprinkle on cheese and roll up into a log shape. Slice and toast immediately, or wrap (unsliced log) in plastic and freeze. When ready to eat, remove from freezer, slice into 4–6 pieces, and toast for a few minutes until golden brown.

PER SERVING (4 PIZZA BITES, 64G): *Calories 140; Total Fat 5.6g; Fiber 1.2g; Total Carbohydrates 18.0g; Sugars 1.6g; Protein 6.0g; Sodium 360mg, Cholesterol 8.0mg Calcium 112mg.*

Lunch Box Muffins— Mac 'n' Cheese Flavor

These are a handy lunch box alternative to sandwiches for kids who are tired of sandwiches or, like mine, just won't eat them! The Sneaky Chef mac 'n' cheese formula is tried-and-true, and this turns it into a handheld meal that can be popped into the kids' lunch boxes. No fork is needed, as they are eaten just like a muffin. (For some reason, children prefer to give up flatware whenever they can and eat with their hands.) Kids don't mind them cold. Make ahead and freeze, take them out and put into the fridge the night before, and you are set to go.

MAKES 8 MUFFINS

4 large eggs

1 cup Orange Puree (see Make-Ahead Recipe #2, p. 44)

2 cups cooked macaroni

2 cups shredded low-fat cheese (Colby or cheddar)

Salt and freshly ground pepper, to taste

Below are two ways to cook the muffins:

Oven baked method:

Preheat oven to 350 degrees and line a muffin tin with paper liners. Lightly spray liners with oil.

In a mixing bowl, whisk the eggs and Orange Puree. Mix in the macaroni and 1½ cups of the cheese. Divide the mixture evenly among the 8 muffin cups. Top each with about 1 tablespoon of cheese and bake for 20 to 22 minutes, until the cheese is lightly browned and bubbly on top. Season with salt and pepper, to taste.

Microwave method:

Line 8 microwave-safe ramekins or custard cups with paper muffin liners. Lightly spray liners with oil.

In a mixing bowl, whisk the eggs and Orange Puree. Mix in the macaroni and 1½ cups of the cheese. Divide the mixture evenly among the 8 lined ramekins. Top each with about 1 tablespoon of cheese and microwave on high for 3 minutes. Season with salt and pepper, to taste.

PER SERVING (1 MUFFIN, 116G): *Calories 155; Total Fat 4.8g; Fiber 1.4g; Total Carbohydrates 15.1g; Sugars 1.8g; Protein 12.3g; Sodium 226mg, Cholesterol 111mg; Calcium 197mg.*

Lunch Box Mexican Muffins

These are inspired by the mac 'n' cheese muffin, and they also make for a delicious Mexican breakfast on the run. I gave this recipe to a few girlfriends to test, and it's become as popular with us adults as it is with the kids.

MAKES 12 MUFFINS

12 (6-inch) round flour tortillas
   (ideally whole wheat)

8 egg whites

4 large eggs

1 cup salsa

1 cup Orange or White Puree (see Make-Ahead Recipe #2, p. 44 or #4, p. 48)

2 cups shredded low-fat cheese
   (Jack or cheddar)

Salt and freshly ground pepper, to taste

Optional Extra Boost: ½ cup chopped sweet
   peppers and/or onions

Below are two ways to cook the muffins:

Oven baked method:

Preheat oven to 350 degrees. Spray both sides of each tortilla lightly with oil, then gently press one tortilla into each muffin tin, making bowl shapes.

In a mixing bowl, whisk the egg whites, eggs, salsa, Orange or White Puree, and 1 cup of the cheese. Divide the mixture evenly among the 8 tortilla cups. Top each evenly with the remaining cheese and bake for 20 to 22 minutes, until the cheese is lightly browned and bubbly on top.

Microwave method:

Spray 8 microwave-safe ramekins or custard cups with oil, then spray both sides of each tortilla lightly with oil. Gently press one tortilla into each ramekin, making bowl shapes.

In a mixing bowl, whisk the egg whites, eggs, salsa, Orange or White Puree, and ¾ cup of the cheese. Divide the mixture evenly among the 8 tortilla cups. Top each with about 1 tablespoon of cheese and microwave on high for 3 minutes. Season with salt and pepper, to taste.

PER SERVING (1 MUFFIN, 128G): *Calories 179; Total Fat 5.4g; Fiber 1.8g; Total Carbohydrates 20.1g; Sugars 2.5g; Protein 12.1g; Sodium 507mg, Cholesterol 74mg; Calcium 197mg.*

Honey-Battered Popcorn Shrimp

This is a great intro to fish for kids. Aside from tuna sandwiches, most kids will normally only go for popcorn shrimp if it's battered and deep-fried so there's no hint of anything fishy lurking beneath. This healthier version gets a nice faux-fried crispiness from the oat bran and cornmeal breading.

MAKES 4 APPETIZER SERVINGS

¼ cup whole-grain flour

2 egg whites

2 tablespoons honey

½ cup oat bran

½ cup cornmeal

1 tablespoon sugar

¼ teaspoon salt

1 pound cleaned, raw rock shrimp
   or small shrimp, shelled and deveined*

2 lemons, cut into wedges

*If using frozen shrimp, defrost for a few minutes in a bowl of cool water, then pat dry

Dipping Sauce:

1 tablespoon honey mustard

1 tablespoon strawberry or apricot jam

2 tablespoons Orange Puree

   (see Make-Ahead Recipe #2, p. 44)

Preheat oven to 425 degrees and spray a baking sheet with oil.

Pour flour into a large plastic bag or onto a plate. Beat egg whites with honey in a shallow bowl and place next to the flour. Combine the oat bran, cornmeal, sugar, and salt in another large plastic bag or shallow bowl. Mix well.

First dredge (or shake in the bag) a small batch of shrimp in the flour and shake off the excess, then dip in the egg mixture, and then dredge (or shake in the bag) in the oat bran mixture.

Place breaded shrimp on the prepared baking sheet. Spray the top side of the shrimp generously with oil and bake for about 6 minutes. With a spatula, turn shrimp over once, spray this side with oil, and then return to oven for another 6 minutes until the coating is lightly browned and crisp.

Serve with lemon wedges and dipping sauce.

For the dipping sauce:
In a small bowl, whisk together all the ingredients. Use immediately, or cover and store in the refrigerator for up to 3 days.

PER SERVING (242G): *Calories 308; Total Fat 2.9g; Fiber 6.7g; Total Carbohydrates 48.5g; Sugars 15.8g; Protein 30.6g; Sodium 442mg; Cholesterol 20mg; Calcium 94mg.* 33% less calories, 84% less fat, 164% more fiber, 36% less sodium, and 14% less sugars than traditional recipe.

Hamburger-Stuffed Potatoes

For the meat-and-potato lover in your kid, this is a full meal in a potato boat. It combines the concept of double stuffed potatoes with a cheeseburger, offering ample opportunities for Sneaky Chefs to slip in some nutritious purees. Prep ahead, refrigerate, then simply heat through at dinnertime (I heat mine in a toaster oven).

MAKES 6 SERVINGS

3 large russet potatoes

For the hamburger mixture:

1 tablespoon olive oil

½ pound lean ground beef or turkey*

1 tablespoon ketchup

1 teaspoon Worcestershire Sauce

3 tablespoons tomato paste

¼ **cup Green Puree (see Make-Ahead Recipe #3, p. 46)**

1 tablespoon oat bran

¼ teaspoon salt

Freshly ground pepper, to taste

For the potato:

1 tablespoon unsalted butter

2 tablespoons plain low-fat yogurt

¼ teaspoon salt

3 slices American cheese, for optional
   variation

Time-saving tip: if you have leftover meat sauce or meatballs on hand, use either as a substitute.

Preheat oven to 450 degrees. Prick potatoes several times with a fork and place them directly on oven rack. Bake for 50 to 60 minutes until tender.

While potatoes are baking, heat the oil over medium heat in a deep skillet or earthenware pot. Add the beef (or turkey), stirring to break it up, and cook for about 5 minutes, until the meat is no longer red. Stir in the ketchup, Worcestershire Sauce, tomato paste, Green Puree, oat bran, salt, and a few grinds of pepper. Mix well. Bring to a boil, and then reduce heat to low and simmer for 10 to 15 minutes.

Remove potatoes from the oven and set aside until cool enough to handle. Cut potatoes in half lengthwise and carefully scoop out the flesh into a mixing bowl, leaving some potato in the skin to keep shells intact. Mash potatoes lightly with a fork, adding the butter, yogurt, and salt. Set aside.

Fill each potato shell with about 2 tablespoons of the cooked hamburger mixture, then top with about 3 tablespoons of the potato mixture, mounding slightly. Spray tops with oil and place back in the oven for 5 minutes, to crisp the top of the potato. Serve immediately.

Cheeseburger variation:

Follow same instructions for Hamburger Stuffed Potato above, adding one-half slice of American cheese to completed stuffed potato half and returning to oven for 5 minutes, until cheese is melted.

PER SERVING (½ POTATO, 261G): *Calories 264; Total Fat 8.3g; Fiber 4.9g; Total Carbohydrates 36.4g; Sugars 3.7g; Protein 12.4g; Sodium 433mg; Cholesterol 29mg; Calcium 94mg.* 25% less fat, 48% less cholesterol, 58% more fiber, 15% more potassium, and 30% less sugars than traditional recipe.

Tijuana Lasagna

Corn tortillas make this dish infinitely easier (and more nutritious) than lasagna noodles that need to be pre-boiled. Plus the layers of ground beef, salsa, and cheese offer a superb hiding place for many sneaky purees.

MAKES 6 SERVINGS

For the ground meat mixture:

1 tablespoon extra-virgin olive oil

1 medium-size onion, finely chopped (about 1½ cups)

1 pound lean ground beef or turkey (or mix both), crumbled

¾ cup salsa

½ **cup Purple, Orange, or White Puree (see Make-Ahead Recipe #1, p. 43, #2, p. 44, or #4, p. 48)**

¼ cup wheat germ

Salt and freshly ground pepper, to taste

4 (6-inch) round corn tortillas (white or yellow)

1 cup shredded low-fat cheddar or Jack cheese

Salt and freshly ground pepper, to taste

Optional Extra Boost: **1 cup each corn and/or black beans**

For the sauce:

¼ **cup Orange Puree (see Make-Ahead Recipe #2, p. 44)**

¾ cup salsa

½ teaspoon each cumin and chili powder

Sneaky Tip:

A tip from my doctor friend Tassos K.—a sneaky trick for cutting onions without burning your eyes is to soak the onion (halved) in salted water for a few minutes before chopping. It takes the sting out!

Preheat oven to 350 degrees and spray a 9- or 10-inch glass pie pan with oil.

Heat the oil over medium heat in a deep skillet or earthenware pot. Add the onions and cook until they are slightly translucent, about 10 minutes. Add the beef (or turkey), stirring to break it up, and cook for about 5 minutes, until the meat is no longer red. Stir in the salsa, puree, wheat germ, a few grinds of pepper, and corn and beans, if using. Bring to a boil, and then reduce heat to low and simmer for 5 to 10 more minutes. While the meat mixture is simmering, mix the Orange Puree, salsa, cumin, and chili powder in a separate mixing bowl.

To assemble the lasagna:

1] Spread ½ cup of sauce on the bottom (center) of the prepared pie plate.

2] Place 1 tortilla on top of the sauce.

3] Spread ½ cup of the meat mixture evenly over the tortilla.

4] Sprinkle ¼ cup of cheese over the meat mixture.

5] Place another tortilla on top of the cheese, then repeat steps 3 and 4 two more times.

6] Finish by topping with remaining tortilla and spread the remaining sauce over the top of the tortilla, then sprinkle with the remaining cheese.

7] Cover lasagna with foil sprayed with oil. Bake 15 minutes. Uncover. Bake another 5 minutes or until the top is lightly browned. Let stand a few minutes before cutting.

PER SERVING (252G): *Calories 290; Total Fat 12.3g; Fiber 4.2g; Total Carbohydrates 22.4g; Sugars 5.3g; Protein 23.5g; Sodium 584mg; Cholesterol 53mg; Calcium 140mg.* 41% less calories, 58% less fat, 35% less cholesterol, 34% less carbs, and 83% more fiber than traditional recipe.

Enlightened Enchiladas

Mexican food takes a close second to Italian cuisine when it comes to recipes offering great hiding places for sneaky ingredients. If only I could feel this good about ordering enchiladas at our neighborhood Mexican restaurant!

MAKES 6 SERVINGS

1 tablespoon olive oil

1 pound lean ground beef or turkey

2 cups store-bought tomato sauce

¾ cup **White or Orange Puree (see Make-Ahead Recipe #4, p. 48 or #2, p. 44)**

1 to 2 tablespoons chili powder

¼ teaspoon *each* cumin, garlic powder, and onion powder

½ cup **Green Puree (see Make-Ahead Recipe #3, p. 46)**

1½ cups shredded low-fat cheddar or Jack cheese

Freshly ground pepper, to taste

6 (8- to 10-inch) flour tortillas, ideally whole wheat

Optional Dipping Sauce: salsa and low-fat sour cream or plain (ideally "Greek") yogurt

Preheat oven to 400 degrees and spray an 11-by-7 (or 2-quart) glass or ceramic baking dish with oil.

Heat the oil over medium heat in a non-stick skillet. Add the beef (or turkey), stirring to break it up, and cook for about 5 minutes, until the meat is no longer red. Meanwhile, in a medium mixing bowl, combine the tomato sauce, White or Orange Puree, chili powder, cumin, garlic powder, and onion powder.

Stir the Green Puree, 1 cup of the red sauce mixture, and ½ cup of the cheese into the skillet with browned meat. Simmer for another 5 minutes.

Spoon meat mixture evenly into tortillas. Coat the bottom of the baking dish with a ladle of sauce mixture. Roll up filled tortillas and place seam-side down in one layer in the prepared baking dish. Pour remaining sauce over the top and sprinkle with remaining cheese.

Cook, uncovered, for 15 to 20 minutes or until cheese is lightly browned and bubbly.

Serve with salsa and plain yogurt or low-fat sour cream, if desired.

PER SERVING (1 ENCHILADA, 306G): *Calories 478; Total Fat 17.7g; Fiber 5.3g; Total Carbohydrates 49.3g; Sugars 7.0g; Protein 30.1g; Sodium 1132mg; Cholesterol 55mg; Calcium 250mg.* 20% less fat, 46% less cholesterol, and 85% more fiber than traditional recipe.

"Every night at the dinner table I snicker as I watch my family eat things they would refuse if served outright."

—Shannon W., Spring Grove, IL (mother of 4)

Surprise Cheese Fries

The Canadians call these national favorite fries with cheese sauce "Poutines,"— but I'll bet they're not slipping cauliflower into them north of the border!

MAKES 4 SERVINGS

1 tablespoon olive oil

2 russet potatoes
   (about 1 pound)

1 tablespoon cornstarch

1 tablespoon cornmeal

Salt and freshly ground
   pepper, to taste

For the cheese sauce:

3 ounces American cheese

¼ cup White Puree
   (see Make-Ahead
   Recipe #4, p. 48)

Preheat the oven to 400 degrees. Rub a baking sheet with the olive oil.

Cut each potato into 8 wedges or several thin sticks and place them in a mixing bowl. Dust with cornstarch and cornmeal, then toss to coat evenly. Spread them in a single layer on the oiled baking sheet. Spray the potatoes generously with oil. Bake for 30 minutes, use a spatula to flip them, and return them to the oven for another 10 to 15 minutes, until crispy and golden brown. Season with salt and pepper to taste.

To Make the Cheese Sauce:

Put the cheese in a microwave-safe bowl. Cover the top of the bowl with a wet paper towel and microwave on high for 30 seconds at a time until fully melted. Stir in White Puree and serve hot.

Alternatively, you can cook the mixture over a double boiler or in a metal bowl over a pot of boiling water. This sauce thickens as it cools, so if there is a delay in serving it, simply put it back in the microwave for another 15 to 30 seconds.

Serve fries with hot cheese sauce on the side or drizzled over the potatoes.

Goes well with Sneaky Sliders, page 141.

PER SERVING (154G): *Calories 198; Total Fat 8.7g; Fiber 2.8g; Total Carbohydrates 24.1g; Sugars 1.2g; Protein 6.7g; Sodium 216mg; Cholesterol 13mg; Calcium 123mg.* 50% less cholesterol, 88% less sodium, and 43% less sugars than traditional recipe.

Speedy Stovetop Lasagna

This has become one of my family's favorite Sneaky Chef dishes. I'm thrilled because it's way easier and much faster to make than the traditional layered lasagna, which I would not normally take the time to make on a weeknight! The key here is to be inexact and trust that the result will taste just as good as "neat" lasagna, which gets just as messy after the first bite anyway. As Michele, a reader, suggested, feel free to improvise and add Orange and White Puree as well.

MAKES 6 SERVINGS

1 tablespoon extra-virgin olive oil

1 medium-size onion, finely chopped
   (about 1½ cups)

3 to 4 garlic cloves, finely minced

1 pound lean ground turkey or beef

¾ cup Green Puree (see Make-Ahead
   Recipe #3, p. 46)

1 can (6-ounces) tomato paste

¼ cup oat bran

½ teaspoon *each* dried basil and oregano

9-ounce box *uncooked* lasagna noodles,
   roughly broken into strips

1 jar (24–26 ounces) marinara sauce

1 cup part-skim shredded mozzarella

Heat the oil over medium heat in a deep skillet or earthenware pot. Add the onions and garlic and cook until they are slightly translucent, about 10 minutes. Add the turkey (or beef), stirring to break it up, and cook for about 5 minutes, until the meat is no longer red. In a medium bowl, combine the Green Puree and tomato paste until the mixture turns brownish in color. Add to skillet and stir in the oat bran, basil, and oregano. Add broken noodles on top of meat mixture, then top with tomato sauce. Fill the empty tomato sauce jar three-quarters full of water (about 2½ cups) and add to skillet. Stir to combine. Bring to boil and then reduce to simmer, cover, and cook for 30 minutes, stirring occasionally. Add cheese on top and do *not* stir again; cover for 3 to 5 minutes until cheese is melted. Serve hot.

PER SERVING (340G): *Calories 528; Total Fat 15.8g; Fiber 7.4g; Total Carbohydrates 82.1g; Sugars 19.1g; Protein 31.1g; Sodium 1380mg; Cholesterol 32mg; Calcium 377mg.* 30% less calories, 60% less fat, 62% less cholesterol, 34% less sodium, and 175% more fiber than traditional recipe.

"Thank you for giving me an opportunity to feed my children healthy food in this fast-food world!"

—Angela M., La Porte, TX (mother of 2)

Sneaky Sliders

These sneaky sliders were inspired by the White Castle fast-food chain, which introduced them in 1921. Sliders have seen a resurgence in high-end restaurants because of their cuteness factor and versatility. These lovable mini-burgers offer a great way to hide maximum nutrients.

MAKES 12 MINI-BURGERS

½ cup **Lentil or Green Puree (see Make-Ahead Recipe #5, p. 50 or #3, p. 46)**

1 tablespoon ketchup

¼ cup **wheat germ**

½ teaspoon salt

1 teaspoon onion powder

1 pound lean ground beef

12 small soft dinner rolls (ideally whole wheat)

Optional Garnish: cheese, pickles, lettuce, and/or ketchup

In a large bowl, mix Lentil or Green Puree, ketchup, wheat germ, salt, and onion powder. Then add the ground beef, mixing with hands until well combined. If too sticky, add a bit more wheat germ.

Using damp hands, shape mixture into 12 small patties, about ½ inch thick. Freeze for future use (within 3 months) or proceed to cook immediately.

Spray a large skillet or grill pan with nonstick cooking spray and set over moderately high heat until hot but not smoking. Cook the burgers for 2 to 3 minutes on each side, then flip and add cheese (if using) to melt over patties for another minute.

Cut dinner rolls horizontally in half and lightly toast. Serve mini-burgers on rolls and garnish with pickles, lettuce, and ketchup, if using.

> **PER SERVING (2 SLIDERS, 174G):** *Calories 402; Total Fat 15.4g; Fiber 8.4g; Total Carbohydrates 45.0g; Sugars 7.2g; Protein 23.4g; Sodium 706mg; Cholesterol 90mg. 48% less fat, 38% less cholesterol, 52% more potassium, and 452% more fiber than traditional recipe.*

Life's Funny Moments Blog

Do you fight with your kids to eat healthy? Yeah . . . me too. Okay. Be honest here. Do you fight with your husband to eat healthy? Be really honest with me. I won't tell. Yeah . . . well, me too. So, what am I going to do? Live the next 15 years fighting with the boys to eat healthy? Um, no thanks. I vividly remember my sister sitting for hours in front of a plate of green beans refusing to eat them. Yum. Nothing better than cold green beans. And she sat there. And sat there. And sat there. She must have given in because she eventually left the table—grew up and moved to Virginia! LOL. Oh, man. I don't want to do that— watch my kids sit there for hours staring at their veggies, which will petrify and turn into a science project right in front of them. So, time to figure out something else. After all . . . I am at war. At least that's what it feels like at night when they eat dinner. I have broken them down about as far as possible without having a complete revolt on my hands.

I'm in the trenches. I found a book that has opened my options. The author is brilliant. She purees healthy food (veggies, fruits, and whole grains) and incorporates them into recipes. She is a warrior. She won the battle. And shared her war plan.

I made the chocolate chip cookies last night. My kids loved them! They are a cross between an oatmeal cookie and a chocolate chip cookie. And, just what the heck are in them, you ask? So glad that you asked. Navy beans, wheat germ, and whole-wheat flour are the basic sneaky ingredients. Both boys gave the cookies a thumbs-up.

And for dinner tomorrow night? Pasta and meatballs. I made the meatballs tonight and the boys tried one, loved it, and asked for more. They are yummy. And the best part? They have peas, carrots, and wheat germ in them. I'd love some more variations on pasta and ground meat recipes.

Excerpted from lifesfunnymoments.blogspot.com
by Kim E., Fredericksburg, VA (mother of 2)

Macaroni 'n' Beef Skillet

This is a one-dish wonder using lentils to replace some of the meat while adding a long-lasting source of energy, protein, fiber, and iron. All your kids will see and taste is their favorite pasta and ground beef, but you'll know there are five super veggies and legumes.

MAKES 6 SERVINGS

1 tablespoon olive oil

1 medium-size onion, finely chopped
   or pureed (about 1½ cups)

½ pound lean ground beef or turkey

1 to 2 cloves garlic, minced

1 cup **Orange or White Puree (see Make-Ahead Recipe #2, p. 44 or #4, p. 48)**

1 cup marinara sauce

½ cup **Lentil Puree (see Make-Ahead Recipe #5, p. 50)**

1 cup chicken or vegetable broth

2 cups *uncooked* macaroni

Salt and freshly ground pepper, to taste

Grated Parmesan cheese, optional

Heat the oil over medium heat in a deep skillet or earthenware pot. Add the onions and cook until they are slightly translucent, about 10 minutes; add the beef (or turkey), stirring to break it up, and cook for about 5 minutes, until the meat is no longer red. Stir in the garlic, Orange or White Puree, marinara sauce, Lentil Puree, broth, and macaroni.

Bring to a boil, then reduce heat to medium-low, cover, and simmer for 20 to 30 minutes, or until pasta is tender.

Season with salt, freshly ground pepper, and grated Parmesan, to taste.

PER SERVING (214G): *Calories 405; Total Fat 7.5g; Fiber 5.6g; Total Carbohydrates 63.5g; Sugars 4.0g; Protein 19.8g; Sodium 181mg; Cholesterol 24mg; Calcium 37mg.* 60% less fat, 70% less cholesterol, 150% more fiber, and 50% less sugars than traditional recipe.

Mexican Cheeseburgers

You can reduce the fat of basic burgers by using lentil puree to add fiber and great nutrition, and the lentil color and flavor disappears like magic. This can be prepared a day ahead and kept covered in the refrigerator.

MAKES 6 KID-SIZED BURGERS

½ cup Lentil Puree (see Make-Ahead Recipe #5, p. 50)

¼ cup salsa

¼ cup wheat germ

½ teaspoon cumin

¼ cup chopped jalapeño peppers, optional

1 pound lean ground beef or turkey

6 slices low-fat Monterey Jack or cheddar cheese, optional

6 hamburger buns or English muffins (ideally whole grain)

Optional Garnish: tomato and/or avocado slices, salsa

In a large bowl, mix Lentil Puree, salsa, wheat germ, cumin, and jalapeños (if using). Then add the ground beef (or turkey), mixing with hands until well combined. If too sticky, add a bit more wheat germ.

Using damp hands, shape mixture into 6 patties. The burgers may be prepared to this point a day ahead and kept covered in the refrigerator.

Spray a large skillet or grill pan with nonstick cooking spray and set over moderately high heat until hot but not smoking. Cook the burgers for 3 minutes on each side, then flip and add cheese (if using) to melt over patties for another 3 minutes.

Serve on fresh, soft burger buns or English muffins with avocado, and tomato slices, and salsa, if using.

PER SERVING (1 BURGER, 169G): *Calories 346; Total Fat 12.0g; Fiber 3.9g; Total Carbohydrates 29.2g; Sugars 3.3g; Protein 29.1g; Sodium 575mg; Cholesterol 55mg; Calcium 283mg.*

"If I didn't know what I was putting in the recipes I would swear they were bad for us because it all tastes so good!"

—*Kelly J., Otsego, MN (mother of 3)*

Fabulous Fried Rice

My kids love to order in Chinese food, but it takes 45 minutes to arrive, is expensive, and has way too much sodium. I think they just love the box it comes in best! Try saving (or buying) some containers and serving it homemade. Make a batch of brown rice to use for the week. This is a great use of leftover rice, chicken, and veggies; in fact, cold cooked leftover rice is key to good fried rice. Use light soy sauce to give it an authentic flavor.

MAKES 6 SERVINGS

2 tablespoons canola, vegetable, or olive oil

3 large eggs

½ cup White Puree (see Make-Ahead
   Recipe #4, p. 48)

1 small onion, minced or pureed

1 to 2 cloves garlic, minced

2 teaspoons fresh ginger, minced
   (or ⅛ teaspoon ground ginger)

2 cups (approximately 12 ounces) cooked,
   cubed chicken, ham, pork, beef, or shrimp

4 cups cooked rice, cold (ideally brown rice)

2 tablespoons low-sodium soy sauce

Salt and freshly ground pepper, to taste

Optional Extra Boost: ½ cup peas and/or
   2 diced scallions

Heat 1 tablespoon of the oil in a large nonstick skillet or wok over medium heat. In a large mixing bowl, whisk eggs with White Puree. Add egg mixture to skillet and scramble quickly until almost set, then transfer egg to the bowl.

Increase heat to medium high and heat remaining oil. Add the onion, garlic, and ginger and stir-fry for about 2 minutes. Spray the skillet with oil, if needed. Add the cubed meat (or shrimp) and stir-fry for another 2 minutes. Add the rice and soy sauce and toss until the ingredients are combined well and the rice is heated through. Allow the rice to brown in the skillet before stirring. Add eggs, peas, and scallion (if using) for the last minute of cooking.

PER SERVING (250G): *Calories 317; Total Fat 8.2g; Fiber 0.9g; Total Carbohydrates 38.4g; Sugars 1.2g; Protein 20.6g; Sodium 277mg, Cholesterol 140mg; Calcium 34mg.*

Wizard's Wonton Soup

This recipe is a labor of love (but less labor than I thought it would be) and is no harder to make than a meatball. This is a great weekend project (with help from the kids). Remember: you don't have to make a perfect triangle; just be sure it is closed. Make these wontons ahead and freeze, uncooked, for up to three months.

MAKES 4 SERVINGS

For the broth:

4 cups chicken broth, ideally low-sodium

1-inch piece of fresh ginger (or ¼ teaspoon ground ginger)

2 teaspoons low-sodium soy sauce

2 dashes sesame oil

Salt and freshly ground pepper, to taste

For the wontons:

¼ cup Green Puree (see Make-Ahead Recipe #3, p. 46)

2 tablespoons pomegranate juice

1 tablespoon low-sodium soy sauce

1 teaspoon fresh grated ginger (or ¼ teaspoon ground ginger)

1 clove of garlic, minced

½ pound ground turkey, lean beef, or pork

16 to 20 wonton wrappers

Optional Extra Boost: 4 green onions, slivered (about ½ cup)

Place broth, piece of ginger, soy sauce, and sesame oil in a large saucepan or soup pot and set the pan over medium-high heat. Bring to a boil and allow broth to simmer while you assemble the wontons.

In a large mixing bowl, combine Green Puree with pomegranate juice until mixture turns a brownish color. Add in soy sauce, ginger, garlic, and ground meat.

Lay out several wonton wrappers on the counter. Fill a small bowl with water and place it near you. Dip your fingertips in the water and use them to brush all of the edges of each wrapper. Place a bite-sized piece of meat mixture (about 1½ teaspoons) in the center of each wrapper. Bring two corners of the wrapper together, forming an *imperfect* triangle. Press the wet edges together to seal.

Using a spoon, gently place wontons in the simmering broth. Add green onions to broth, if using. Return to boil and simmer for 10 minutes. Wontons are fully cooked when they float to the top of the broth. Remove the piece of ginger from the broth and gently ladle wontons with broth into soup bowls. Season with salt to taste.

PER SERVING (351G): *Calories 232; Total Fat 5.5g; Fiber 1.2g; Total Carbohydrates 28.1g; Sugars 2.3g; Protein 20.8g; Sodium 785mg; Cholesterol 36mg; Calcium 37mg.* 44% less calories, 48% less fat, 44% less cholesterol, 44% less carbs, and 35% less sugars than traditional recipe.

Short-Order Cook Needs Help

Dear Sneaky Chef,

I'm sure I'm somehow to blame. Let's not get into HOW this happened, as it would take up way too much of your time. Suffice it to say, I feel like a short-order cook, and need a "one-meal solution" to my family's food preferences.

—My husband and daughter don't eat red meat (unless it's bacon!).

—My daughter and son don't eat seafood.

—My husband can't eat dairy. My son should avoid it but loves it.

—Everyone eats chicken but gets tired of it.

—Everyone likes pasta, but it's nutritionally lacking (no takers on whole grain).

—They all eat beans from time to time, though my son does not like the complimentary rice (my daughter likes plain white rice with lots of butter).

With two teenagers and a husband who all keep odd schedules in addition to their pet peeves, I find myself alternately spending too much time on my feet in the kitchen trying to be all things to all people at all hours, or not trying at all. Reaching for my wallet and pointing my family toward the local pizza joint up the block would be the perfect solution except that my husband doesn't eat pizza!

I'm writing to see if you can help make my dream of family mealtime a reality. Primarily, I'm seeking recipes that will keep chicken and pasta interesting day after day after day while providing a lot of flavor, variety, and nutrition. Thanks!

—Jinny B., Marblehead, NY (mother of 2)

Lucky Lo Mein

The Chinese have countless variations of "chicken and pasta" that will keep any family interested. Normally, lo mein is one of the highest fat and least nutritious Chinese entrees. In some Chinese restaurants, a serving can contain more than 100 grams of fat! Here's a sneaky alternative that's quicker and cheaper than take-out—and has a fraction of the fat.

MAKES 4 SERVINGS

3 tablespoons low-sodium soy sauce

½ cup White Puree (see Make-Ahead Recipe #4, p. 48)

½ cup vegetable or chicken broth, ideally low-sodium

1½ teaspoons toasted sesame oil

1 teaspoon fresh grated ginger (or ¼ teaspoon ground ginger)

1 tablespoon canola or vegetable oil

½ pound thin spaghetti or lo mein noodles, cooked (ideally whole wheat)

8 ounces shredded chicken (approximately 1½ cups)

Optional Extra Boost: ½ cup each long, thinly sliced carrots, bell peppers, and/or snow peas

Salt to taste

In a large mixing bowl, whisk together the soy sauce, White Puree, broth, sesame oil, and ginger.

Heat oil in a large nonstick skillet or wok over medium heat. If using optional extra veggies, add them to the skillet and stir-fry for about 3 minutes. Add cooked noodles and sauce to the skillet and toss to evenly coat the noodles. Serve hot in Chinese take-out containers with chopsticks!

PER SERVING (168G): *Calories 349; Total Fat 8.3g; Fiber 2.4g; Total Carbohydrates 45.1g; Sugars 1.9g; Protein 15.6g; Sodium 577mg; Cholesterol 25mg; Calcium 24mg. 41% less fat, 73% less cholesterol, 50% less sodium, 46% less carbs, and 68% less sugars than traditional recipe.*

Sweet 'n' Sassy Meatballs

I've heard from many mothers that the reason their children won't eat meat is that it's too hard to chew. Meatballs' soft texture eases kids into meat products, since they're not sinewy and unchewable. If you want a sweet and tangy alternative to the traditional Italian version, try these sweet and sour meatballs, either simmered in sauce or simply eaten off a toothpick.

MAKES 18 MEATBALLS

1 large egg, beaten

2 to 3 cloves garlic, minced

½ teaspoon ground ginger

½ **cup Orange Puree (See Make-Ahead Recipe #2, p. 44)**

2 tablespoons jam (strawberry, grape, or seedless raspberry, no sugar added)

2 tablespooons ketchup

¼ teaspoon salt

¾ cup wheat germ

1 pound lean ground beef or turkey

2 tablespoons extra-virgin olive oil, for baking meatballs (4 tablespoons oil for pan-fry method)

In a large bowl, whisk together egg, garlic, ginger, orange puree, jam, ketchup, salt, and wheat germ, mixing well. Add the ground meat and mix with hands until well combined. Using damp hands, pinch off a large tablespoon of meat and gently shape mixture into golf ball–sized meatballs.

Below are two ways to cook the meatballs, depending on fat restrictions and how much time you have. The oven method is lower in fat and quicker, and the result is nearly as good as the pan frying.

GRILLED CHEESE AND TOMATO SOUP

Sneaky ingredients: White beans, carrots, yams, cauliflower, and zucchini

**LUNCH BOX
BISCUITS**

Sneaky ingredients:
Whole wheat,
wheat germ,
cauliflower,
 zucchini

**SNEAKY
SLIDERS WITH
CHOCOLATE
EGG CREAMS
AND SURPRISE
CHEESE FRIES**

*Sneaky ingredients
(sliders):* Lentils
and wheat germ
*Sneaky ingredients
(egg cream):*
Cherries
*Sneaky ingredients
(fries):* Cauliflower,
zucchini

BBQ: PULLED BBQ CHICKEN, BBQ SAUCE, AND MIGHTY TOTS

Sneaky ingredients (BBQ Chicken): Cauliflower, zucchini, carrots, yams

Sneaky ingredients (Tots): White beans, oat bran

FABULOUS FRIED RICE

Sneaky ingredients: Cauliflower, zucchini, onions, whole grain brown rice

WIZARD WONTON SOUP

Sneaky ingredients: Spinach, broccoli, peas, pomegranate

STUFFED SHELLS, ITALIAN WEDDING SOUP, SPEEDY STOVETOP LASAGNE

Sneaky ingredients (stuffed shells): Wheat germ, cauliflower, zucchini

Sneaky ingredients (wedding soup): Spinach, broccoli, peas, oat bran

Sneaky ingredients (Speedy Stovetop Lasagna): Spinach, broccoli, peas, whole wheat, and oat bran

LUCKY LO MEIN

Sneaky ingredients: Cauliflower, zucchini, whole wheat

QUICK FIX FOR YELLOW CAKE MIX

Sneaky ingredients: Carrots, yams, white beans, oat bran

Oven-baked method:

Preheat oven to 350 degrees. Brush a large cookie sheet with 2 tablespoons oil, gently place meatballs on sheet, and bake for 10 minutes. Using a spatula to loosen, turn the meatballs over to brown on the other side, then return to the oven for another 10 minutes. Simmer and serve with Sweet 'n' Sassy Sauce, page _, if desired.

Pan-fry method:

Heat 1 tablespoon of the oil in a large (10- or 12-inch) nonstick skillet over moderately high heat, until hot but not smoking (add cooking spray oil to coat pan as well). Add about 8 meatballs per batch to avoid overcrowding the pan. Allow to brown on all sides for about 5 minutes, turning occasionally with the help of two spoons. Finish cooking through for 10 minutes in a 350 degree oven. Simmer and serve with Sweet 'n' Sassy Sauce (next page), if desired.

PER SERVING, APPROX. 3 MEATBALLS (137G):
Calories 259; Total Fat 13.0g; Fiber 2.6g; Total Carbohydrates 18.0g; Sugars 6.4g; Protein 18.0g; Sodium 155mg; Cholesterol 94mg; Calcium 45mg. 22% less calories, 48% less fat, 69% less sodium, 14% less cholesterol, 36% more potassium, and 310% more fiber than traditional recipe.

Sweet 'n' Sassy Sauce

MAKES ABOUT 2 CUPS OF SAUCE

¼ cup low-sodium
  soy sauce

¼ cup packed brown sugar

**1 cup Orange Puree
(see Make-Ahead
Recipe #2, p. 44)**

½ cup pomegranate juice

2 tablespoons cider vinegar

½ to ¾ teaspoon cayenne
  pepper, optional

1 teaspoon ground ginger

Optional Extra Boost:

  ½ cup pineapple

  chunks

Whisk together all ingredients. Store in refrigerator for up to one week.

> **PER SERVING (¼ CUP, 49G):** *Calories 64; Total Fat 0.1g; Fiber 1.0g; Total Carbohydrates 15.5g; Sugars 11.0; Protein 0.8g; Sodium 288mg; Cholesterol 0mg.* 900% more fiber, and 116% more protein than traditional recipe.

"Now if only you could open

a fast-food Sneaky Chef place,

I would be there all the time!"

—Kara M., Manchester, NH (pregnant mother)

Slow Cooker Pulled BBQ Chicken

The idea behind slow cookers is to have a tender, delicious dinner that's cooking while you're gone and ready when you walk in the door. Chicken and stew recipes are most ideal for this hands-off gadget.

MAKES 6 SERVINGS

1¼ cups store-bought barbeque sauce (or 2 cups Down Under BBQ Sauce, p. 165)*

¾ cup White or Orange Puree (see Make-Ahead Recipe #4, p. 48 or #2, p. 44)

¼ cup vegetable or chicken broth, ideally low-sodium

2 tablespoons oat bran

4 skinless half chicken breasts, with bone (about 2 pounds)

6 hamburger buns or English muffins (ideally whole grain), optional

*If using Down Under BBQ Sauce, use 2 cups of sauce and omit the additional White or Orange Puree in this recipe

In the slow cooker pot, mix BBQ sauce with White or Orange Puree, broth, and oat bran. Add chicken to slow cooker and toss. Cover. Cook 5 hours on low or 2½ hours on high.

Remove chicken from slow cooker. Shred chicken using two forks and toss with the barbeque sauce. Serve on warm hamburger buns or English muffins, if desired.

Note: For best results, do not remove cover during cooking.

PER SERVING (279G): *Calories 339; Total Fat 6.0g; Fiber 3.6g; Total Carbohydrates 21.0g; Sugars 12.4g; Protein 49.7g; Sodium 659mg; Cholesterol 128mg; Calcium 88mg.* 47% less calories, 83% less fat, 21% less cholesterol, 18% less sodium, 94% more potassium, 50% less carbs, 368% more fiber, and 70% less sugar than traditional recipe.

"I Love You Mummy"

I am a mum of six children ranging from nineteen to eight. My three youngest have autism.

Finding food that they will eat is hard enough, but healthy food is even harder. We decided to take out a lot of the preservatives in their diet as well as getting them to eat healthier.

Finding your book was a godsend. While making up the purees, I despaired getting them to eat them. Then I stood in awe as my nine-year-old took off with the bowl that I had made the "Brainy Brownies" in and began to lick it. I can make up food now knowing that in most things they are getting such wonderful vegetables. Putting a white and an orange puree into plain baked beans and watching them eat it is incredible.

My son's teacher came up to me after two weeks and asked me what I had done. She told me that my son was now working alone without needing much help, and his spelling and English had improved dramatically. My nine-year-old daughter is amazing. Since starting with the purees and other things in the book, her speech has improved dramatically and she now has at least twice the number of words. When she got out of the car the other day, and just before she ran off to school, she turned and called out, "I love you mummy." I sat and cried because that is not something she says. If I could meet Missy I would give her the hugest hug because without this book I would definitely not have the kids I have today. Thank you, thank you, thank you for giving my kids back to me.

—Tina E., Australia (mum of 6)

Down Under BBQ Sauce

This recipe is dedicated to Tina E. of Australia, who submitted a beautiful account of how Sneaky Chef recipes have helped her family. I hope this homemade barbecue sauce will be a sneaky staple not only in Tina's home Down Under, but in homes worldwide.

MAKES 2 CUPS OF SAUCE

½ cup vegetable broth

1 cup Orange or White Puree (see Make-Ahead Recipe #2, p. 44 or #4, p. 48)

½ cup cider vinegar

¾ cup tomato paste

¼ teaspoon garlic powder

2 tablespoons Worcestershire sauce

2 tablespoons honey

1 to 2 teaspoons chili powder

Hot sauce to taste

Freshly ground pepper, to taste

Whisk together all ingredients except chili powder, hot sauce, and pepper. Add chili powder, hot sauce, and freshly ground pepper to taste. Thin with more vegetable broth, if desired. Store in the refrigerator for up to 3 days.

PER SERVING (¼ CUP, 47G): *Calories 33; Total Fat 0.17g; Fiber 1.1g; Total Carbohydrates 7.4g; Sugars 4.7g; Protein .82g; Sodium 178mg; Cholesterol 0mg.* 51% less calories, 55% less carbs, 1000% more fiber, 12% more potassium, 143% more protein, and 69% less sugars than traditional recipe.

Retro Tuna Casserole

anti oxidant boost **protein boost** **omega 3s** **low sugar**

This classic recipe, which most Baby Boomers grew up loving and eating frequently, is also a bargain and a handy solution for when your cupboards are a bit bare. We always have a can of tuna or sardines and a little cheese and pasta in the house. When I make this dish, my kids will eat it for breakfast/lunch/dinner for a few days. Sardines significantly upgrade the Omega-3s and calcium without changing the flavor.

MAKES 6 SERVINGS

½ cup White Puree (see Make-Ahead Recipe #4, p. 48)

½ cup evaporated skim milk

½ teaspoon onion powder

1 teaspoon Worcestershire sauce

½ pound egg noodles or elbows, cooked al dente (firm)

1 can (4.37 ounces) skinless and boneless sardines, packed in water, drained

1 can (6 ounces) chunk light tuna, packed in water, drained

1½ cups shredded low-fat Colby or cheddar cheese

Preheat oven to 375 degrees and spray an 11-by-7 (2-quart) glass or ceramic casserole dish with oil.

In the casserole dish, whisk the White Puree, evaporated milk, salt, onion powder, and Worcestershire sauce. Add the pasta, sardines, tuna, and ½ cup of the cheese and mix well. Sprinkle remaining 1 cup cheese evenly over the top of the casserole. Cover with aluminum foil (spray one side with oil so it doesn't stick to the cheese) and bake for 15 minutes. Uncover and continue cooking for another 10 minutes or until lightly browned and bubbly. Serve hot.

PER SERVING (143G): *Calories 188; Total Fat 4.9g; Fiber 0.8g; Total Carbohydrates 13.6g; Sugars 3.3g; Protein 21.4g; Sodium 558mg; Cholesterol 38mg; Calcium 362mg.* 20% less calories, 53% less fat, 111% more potassium, 44% less carbohydrates, and 93% more protein than traditional recipe.

Slow Cooker Purple Chicken

My kids giggled all day long as they passed by the slow cooker simmering with what I told them was "Purple Chicken." I guess it reminded them of something as silly as "green eggs and ham." This recipe practically cooks itself and makes any weeknight family dinner into a special occasion.

MAKES 4 SERVINGS

1 cup Cherry Puree
  (see Make-Ahead
  Recipe #7, p. 52)

1 cup dried cherries or
  cranberries

½ cup pomegranate juice

1 large red onion,
  pureed or diced

½ teaspoon onion powder

1 six-ounce can tomato paste

1 tablespoon olive
  or walnut oil

2 tablespoons oat bran

4 half skinless chicken
  breasts on bone

Salt to taste

In the slow cooker pot, mix Cherry Puree with dried cherries (or cranberries), pomegranate juice, onion, onion powder, tomato paste, oil, and oat bran. Add chicken to slow cooker and toss. Cover. Cook 5 hours on low or 2½ hours on high.

Remove chicken from slow cooker and serve over hot.

Note: For best results, do not remove cover during cooking.

Goes well with Wild Rice, next page.

PER SERVING (375G): *Calories 474; Total Fat 5.4g; Fiber 15.6g; Total Carbohydrates 76.1g; Sugars 51.2g; Protein 32.5g; Sodium 384mg; Cholesterol 68mg; Calcium 39mg. 47% less fat, 42% less cholesterol, 176% more fiber, 33% more potassium, and 46% less sodium than traditional recipe.*

Wild Rice

MAKES 4 SERVINGS

1 cup pomegranate juice

1⅓ cups chicken or
   vegetable broth

1 cup wild rice, ideally
   "quick-cooking"

Salt and freshly ground
   pepper, to taste

Optional Extra Boost:

   ½ cup each dried
   cherries or cranberries
   and chopped walnuts

In a medium saucepan, bring pomegranate juice and broth to a boil, stir in rice, cover, and reduce to simmer on low. Cook for 35 to 40 minutes. Remove from heat and drain off any remaining liquid. Stir in optional extras, if using. Add salt and freshly ground pepper to taste.

PER SERVING (119G): *Calories 195; Total Fat 0.9g; Fiber 2.5g; Total Carbohydrates 40.3g; Sugars 9.2g; Protein 7.5g; Sodium 257mg; Cholesterol 0mg; Calcium 12mg.* 84% less fat, 338% more fiber, and 19% more protein than traditional recipe.

Treasure-Stuffed Shells

"Stuff" your family with great wholesome ingredients and plenty of vegetables when you prepare this easy, everyday dish. My girls devour these every time I make them. It's pure Italian and as easy as ordering in pizza.

MAKES 4 SERVINGS

12 large pasta shells

½ cup part-skim ricotta

¼ cup grated Parmesan cheese

¾ cup White Puree (see Make-Ahead Recipe #4, p. 48)

2 egg whites

3 tablespoons wheat germ

1¼ cups tomato sauce

¾ cups part-skim mozzarella cheese

Preheat oven to 350 degrees and spray an 11-by-7 (or 2-quart) glass or ceramic baking dish with cooking spray.

Cook 12 shells according to package directions until slightly firm. Drain and set aside. Mix ricotta, Parmesan cheese, ¼ cup of the White Puree, egg whites, and wheat germ in a bowl. Combine tomato sauce with remaining White Puree in another bowl.

Pour about ¾ cup of the tomato sauce mixture onto the bottom of the prepared casserole dish. Fill the shells evenly with spoonfuls of the cheese mixture and place them seam side down in casserole dish. Top shells with remaining sauce and the mozzarella cheese.

Cover stuffed shells with foil. Bake 20 minutes. Uncover. Bake for another 10 minutes or until the top is lightly browned.

PER SERVING (3 SHELLS, 230G): *Calories 324; Total Fat 12.0g; Fiber 3.3g; Total Carbohydrates 30.0g; Sugars 3.1g; Protein 24.3g; Sodium 714mg; Cholesterol 42mg; Calcium 265mg. 25% less calories, 23% less sodium, 44% less fat, 16% less carbohydrates, 127% more fiber, 36% less sugars, and 60% less cholesterol than traditional recipe.*

Italian Wedding Soup

When I was researching the traditional ingredients for this recipe, I learned that this soup didn't get its name because it was served at Italian weddings. What it really stands for is the "marriage" between the flavors of the greens and meat. This is an entire meal in a bowl, and it's another make-ahead that you can either freeze or eat all week long.

MAKES 8 SERVINGS

For the meatballs:

¼ cup uncooked bulgur*

1 cup water

1 egg white

¼ cup Green Puree (see Make-Ahead Recipe #3, p. 46)

2 tablespoons tomato paste

2 tablespoons grated Parmesan cheese

½ teaspoon *each* garlic and onion powder

½ pound lean ground beef

If you don't have bulgur, use the same amount of oat bran or wheat germ in the meatballs and use orzo pasta or other small pasta in the soup.

For the soup:

8 cups chicken broth, ideally low-sodium

½ teaspoon *each* garlic powder and onion powder

½ cup uncooked bulgur (or orzo or small star-shaped pasta)

Salt and freshly ground pepper, to taste

2 tablespoons grated Parmesan cheese, optional

Optional Extra Boost: 2 cups thinly sliced escarole or spinach

To make the meatballs:

Place bulgur in a microwave-safe bowl and add the water. Cover bowl with a wet paper towel and microwave on high for 3 to 4 minutes (checking and stirring every minute) until bulgur is soft.

In a large bowl, whisk together the egg white, Green Puree, tomato paste, Parmesan, garlic, onion powder, and softened bulgur. Add the ground meat and mix with your hands until well combined. Using damp hands, pinch off about a teaspoon of the mixture per meatball and gently shape it into tiny (about ½-inch) sized balls. Set meatballs aside until broth is ready.

For the broth:

In a large soup pot, bring broth, garlic powder, and onion powder to a boil over medium-high heat. Add the meatballs, uncooked bulgur (or pasta), and greens, if using, to the boiling broth. Reduce heat to a simmer and cook, stirring occasionally, for 15 minutes. Ladle the soup into bowls and season with salt and freshly ground pepper, to taste. Top with Parmesan cheese, if desired.

PER SERVING (338G): *Calories 119; Total Fat 4.7g; Fiber 1.4g; Total Carbohydrates 6.2g; Sugars 1.6g; Protein 12.7g; Sodium 348mg; Cholesterol 19mg; Calcium 43mg.* 43% less calories, 39% less fat, 70% less cholesterol, 65% less carbs, and 21% less sugars than traditional recipe.

"Every time I use one of your healthy (and sneaky) tips or wonderful recipes, I just want to scream with joy because they eat it"

— Mindi B., Keller, TX (mother of 3)

Clever Chicken Teriyaki

Teriyaki sauce offers a strong, flavorful addition and dark color that acts as the ideal hiding place for most sneaky purees. Unfortunately, the Green Puree failed; I thought it would disappear in the brown teriyaki sauce, but for some reason it didn't. So stick with the lighter-colored White or Orange Purees for best results.

MAKES 4 SERVINGS

2 tablespoons canola or vegetable oil

1 pound boneless, skinless chicken tenders
(or boneless, skinless chicken breasts,
cut into strips)

⅓ cup store-bought teriyaki sauce, ideally
low-sodium

⅓ cup White Puree (see Make-Ahead
Recipe #4, p. 48)

1 tablespoon honey

Optional Extra Boost: 4 green onions, sliced
on diagonal into small pieces and/or
1 cup pineapple chunks.

Heat oil in a large nonstick skillet over medium-high heat. Add chicken to skillet and sauté until no longer pink, about 5 minutes. While chicken is cooking, whisk together the teriyaki sauce, White Puree, and honey. Add teriyaki sauce mixture, green onions, and pineapple chunks, if using, to skillet and toss to coat the chicken. Cook for another 2 minutes. Serve over brown rice or noodles.

PER SERVING (168G): *Calories 226; Total Fat 8.4g; Fiber 0.4g; Total Carbohydrates 8.9g; Sugars 7.8g; Protein 28.0g; Sodium 996mg; Cholesterol 65mg; Calcium 22mg.* 12% less calories, 21% less fat, 17% less cholesterol, 33% less carbs, 19% more fiber, 11% more potassium, 40% less sodium, and 29% less sugars than traditional recipe.

Mighty Tots

Turn a side dish that isn't particularly healthy into a main course filled with whole grains and protein. Make a few batches at a time, then freeze in plastic bags for your own version of frozen tots.

MAKES 4 SERVINGS

2 cups frozen shredded hash browns, thawed and drained

½ cup White Bean Puree (see Make-Ahead Recipe #9, p. 54)

¼ cup oat bran

2 tablespoons canola or vegetable oil

In a medium-size bowl, mix together the hash browns, White Bean Puree, and oat bran. Form teaspoon-size scoops into small balls.

Heat one tablespoon of oil over medium-high heat in a large (10- or 12-inch) nonstick skillet. Reduce the temperature to medium if the oil starts to smoke. Working in batches, carefully drop several tots onto the hot skillet. Reduce heat to medium and pan fry, turning occasionally, until all sides are golden brown, about 3 minutes. Repeat with the next batches of tots, adding more oil to the pan as needed. Place the browned tots on a plate lined with paper towels to blot away excess oil.

Serve immediately, or let cool and store in a plastic bag in the freezer for use within 3 months (simply bake for 20 minutes at 400 degrees when ready to eat).

PER SERVING (½ CUP, 155G): *Calories 224; Total Fat 8.2g; Fiber 4.9g; Total Carbohydrates 34.2g; Sugars 0.1g; Protein 7.0g; Sodium 25mg; Cholesterol 0mg; Calcium 53mg.* 27% less calories, 44% less fat, 42% less cholesterol, 36% more fiber, 27% more potassium, 90% less sodium, 94% more protein, and 95% less sugars than traditional recipe.

*"How can I get healthier stuff into Tater Tots® to make
them into a whole meal with some protein?"*

—Melissa J., Clinton, IA (mother of 1)

Tater Pups

*Kids are immediately attracted to anything they can eat by holding it in their hand. That's part of
the appeal of tater tots and hot dogs. Also, they happen to fall into two of kids' favorite food groups:
potatoes and hot dogs. The availability of frozen shredded hash browns makes this recipe very easy.
White Bean Puree and oat bran act as binders to keep the hot dogs cozily nestled. Use for dinner,
lunch at home, or a "mini-meal" after school.*

MAKES 4 SERVINGS

2 cups frozen shredded hash browns,
    thawed and drained

½ cup White Bean Puree (see Make-Ahead
    Recipe #9, p. 54)

¼ cup whole-wheat flour

4 hot dogs, turkey, beef, or soy (ideally with
    no nitrates), cut into ½-inch pieces

Preheat oven to 425 degrees. Line a baking
sheet with parchment paper (or spray with oil).

In a medium-size bowl, mix together the
hash browns, White Bean Puree, and flour.
Pinch off about one tablespoon of potato dough
mixture and, using hands, press dough to fully
wrap around each piece of hot dog. Form into
log or ball shapes. Spray all sides of the
wrapped hot dog with oil and and bake for 10
minutes. Remove the pan from the oven, flip

the pups, spray the other side with oil, and bake for another 10 minutes. Serve as a hot dish, or let cool and store in a plastic bag in the freezer for use within 3 months (simply toast when ready to eat).

PER SERVING (½ CUP, 210G): *Calories 306; Total Fat 11.9g; Fiber 4.9g; Total Carbohydrates 36.7g; Sugars 0.0g; Protein 14.0g; Sodium 613mg; Cholesterol 23mg; Calcium 59mg.*

TREATS AND DRINK RECIPES

Healthy Sweets Help Comfort Dad

Dear Sneaky Chef,

My father-in-law was hospitalized for an infection of his new heart valve. Not surprisingly, this trauma took a toll on him, and his appetite was not good. Though he needed to be eating more and better food to gain his strength back, he was just not hungry. This troubled us greatly.

Sweets are his favorite, which of course aren't usually the healthiest choice to make under even the best of circumstances, so I put my Sneaky Chef hat on and whipped up some sneakily fortified recipes.

First came sneaky cupcakes, with hidden blueberries, spinach, whole-wheat flour, and wheat germ. They went down easily! So I went on to Sneaky Chef's chocolate pudding with hidden avocado. Another hit! Then I brought out the chocolate chip cookies with hidden white beans, oats, wheat germ, and whole-wheat flour, which were among his favorites. We couldn't have been more pleased.

As a family we felt much better knowing that the "sweets" he was eating to gain his strength back were packed full of healthy ingredients! Please give us more!

— Melissa C., Dallas, TX (daughter-in-law and mother of 1)

Icy Hot Chocolate

I won't even pretend that this comes close to the original recipe for frozen hot chocolate made famous at Serendipity in New York. The restaurant no longer exists, but we can still enjoy the fun of this treat with some super nutrients snuck in. First, our frozen hot "cocoa" uses unsweetened cocoa, which is high in antioxidants and has no fat or sugar; next we boost the calcium content by adding powdered milk to the skim milk base. The final bonus is added taste in the form of chocolate chips in the blender, which leave little tiny bits of yummy chocolate in your mouth!

MAKES 2 SERVINGS

1 cup skim milk

¼ cup semisweet chocolate chips
   (about 2 ounces)

1 tablespoon unsweetened cocoa powder

⅓ cup nonfat dry milk

⅓ cup low-fat vanilla yogurt

1 tablespoon wheat germ

3 to 4 cups ice

Optional Topping: whipped cream

Put all the ingredients in a blender and blend on high until smooth. Serve in a large coffee mug or parfait glass and top with whipped cream, if desired.

PER SERVING (211G): *Calories 277; Total Fat 8.0g; Fiber 2.6g; Total Carbohydrates 39.4g; Sugars 27.5g; Protein 16.3g; Sodium 209mg; Cholesterol 8mg; Calcium 508mg. 24% less calories, 67% less fat, 90% less cholesterol, 146% more potassium, and 151% more protein than traditional recipe.*

"Can you tell me how to make a non-chocolate healthy cake for my son's birthday?"

—Juli B., Vernon Hills, IL (mother of 1)

Monkey Bars

Julie can find healthier, non-chocolate birthday cake recipes on page 184, and I do have another creative solution here which children are particularly fond of. I can't get most of my taste testers to eat banana bread (maybe it seems too healthy), but they gobble up these banana bars because they're more like a soft, square cookie. They especially love it when I drizzle melted white chocolate in thin stripes across the top. When decorated with sprinkles and candles, these bars make a great alternative to birthday cake, plus kids can hold them in their hands.

MAKES 1 DOZEN BARS

5 tablespoons butter

½ cup packed brown sugar

½ teaspoon salt

½ cup Orange Puree (see Make-Ahead Recipe #2, p. 44)

2 large bananas, mashed with the back of a fork (about 1 cup)

1 teaspoon pure vanilla extract

Powdered sugar, for dusting

2 egg yolks

½ cup old-fashioned rolled oats (not quick-cooking)

¾ cup Flour Blend (see Make-Ahead Recipe #10, p. 56)

Optional Decoration: ½ cup white chocolate chips, melted in microwave

Preheat oven to 325 degrees.

Butter or spray only the bottom, not the sides, of an 11-by-7-inch or 9-inch square baking pan. Lightly dust with flour.

In a saucepan over medium-low heat, melt the butter, sugar, and salt. Remove from heat and allow mixture to cool a bit. Once cool, whisk in the Orange Puree, bananas, vanilla, and egg yolks. Add the oats and Flour Blend and mix until just combined. Pour the entire mixture into the prepared baking pan and bake for 37 to 39 minutes, or until a toothpick comes out clean. Allow to cool completely in pan before cutting into approximately 3" bars. If desired, dust with powdered sugar when cool, or drizzle melted white chocolate in a striped pattern across the tops of the bars.

Keeps for a week in the refrigerator, covered tightly.

PER SERVING (1 BAR, 61G): *Calories 151; Total Fat 6.1g; Fiber 1.9g; Total Carbohydrates 22.9g; Sugars 12.2g; Protein 2.5g; Sodium 142mg; Cholesterol 44mg.* 97% more fiber, 68% more potassium, and 17% less sugars than traditional recipe.

They Know What I'm Doing Now and They Love It!

I became interested in The Sneaky Chef when my sister got the first book for Christmas. She made many of the recipes for her children and her husband. The mistake she made was telling them what she was doing. They immediately rejected her cooking. So I learned from her mistake and I kept it all quiet. . . at first.

Now I cook from both books several times a week. My husband and my son know what I'm doing now, and they love it. I can put a smile on my son's face just by saying, "Do you want some sneaky pudding for dessert tonight?" He'll watch me mash up the avocado right in front of him and mix it up in the chocolate pudding, then eat the whole thing. Then he'll laugh as he tells his dad, "I just ate sneaky pudding!" (We actually call that one "chocomole" instead of guacamole!)

I want to tell Ms. Lapine thank you because I was brought up in a household without home-cooked meals. I was never interested in cooking until I had my children. But now, I'm so proud of myself because I feed my children (four-year-old and eight-month old) and my husband healthy meals that come from my heart and my hands. So, thank you, Missy, and would you please create more pudding recipes for us?

—Lisa B., Lilburn, GA (mother of 2)

Racy Rice Pudding

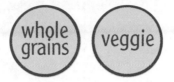

These rice puddings are dedicated to Lisa B. of Lilburn, GA and her family.

MAKES 6 SERVINGS

Vanilla version:

2 cups skim milk

2 cups evaporated skim milk

¼ cup **White Bean Puree (see Make-Ahead Recipe #9, p. 54)**

½ cup sugar

¼ teaspoon salt

½ teaspoon cinnamon

1 teaspoon pure vanilla extract

3½ cups cooked short brown rice (use leftovers if you have them)

In a medium sauce pan, combine skim milk, evaporated milk, White Bean Puree, sugar, salt, cinnamon, and vanilla. Bring to a boil over medium-high heat, stirring frequently. Add rice and reduce to a simmer. Cook for 20 to 30 minutes or until thickened.

PER SERVING (300G): *Calories 296; Total Fat 1.3g; Fiber 2.2g; Total Carbohydrates 58.3g; Sugars 26.4g; Protein 12.5g; Sodium 244mg; Cholesterol 5mg; Calcium 380mg. 34% less calories, 87% less fat, 93% less cholesterol, 27% less carbs, 15% more fiber, 44% more potassium, 19% more protein, and 32% less sugars than traditional recipe.*

Chocolate version:

2 cups skim milk

2 cups evaporated skim milk

¼ cup Cherry Puree (see Make-Ahead
   Recipe #7, p. 52)

½ cup sugar

1 teaspoon cinnamon

¼ teaspoon salt

¼ cup unsweetened cocoa powder

1 teaspoon pure vanilla extract

3½ cups cooked short brown rice
   (use leftovers if you have them)

In a medium saucepan, combine skim milk, evaporated milk, Cherry Puree, sugar, cinnamon, salt, cocoa powder, and vanilla. Bring to a boil over medium-high heat, stirring frequently. Add rice and reduce to a simmer. Cook for 20 to 30 minutes or until thickened.

PER SERVING (314G): *Calories 310; Total Fat 1.9g; Fiber 3.7g; Total Carbohydrates 61.9g; Sugars 28.0g; Protein 13.2g; Sodium 245mg; Cholesterol 5mg; Calcium 387mg.*

Mom of 9 Sneaks 3 Meals Every Day!

I am a mother of nine children who range in age from seven months to eighteen years. We have breakfast, lunch, and dinner at home seven days a week, with the occasional meal out (once a month, on average). I have, therefore, some experience in the kitchen. I love to cook, love to bake, and simply cannot own enough cookbooks. But Missy's Sneaky Chef books aren't my cookbooks; they're my guidebooks.

We have yet to try anything in which the vegetables were detected, or that anyone refused due to taste. Pizza sauce is soooo forgiving—I can add Orange and White Puree, and it works fine. I love the Flour Blend as well, as I bake nearly every day! Spaghetti sauce is another thing that I love, because so many things can be added to it. Lunch often includes boxed macaroni with LOTS of the Orange Puree—no one is the wiser. I recently made chicken Alfredo, a favorite among the children, with White Puree, just to test, and again, no flavor difference. I could have added more, so I will next time.

I have an idea for you—yellow cake mix can become sneaky cupcakes with applesauce, whole grains, and Orange Puree or pureed white beans. If moms would take the time to discover the ways to use these recipes, our children would be so much healthier!

—Mary-Belle S., Staley, NC (mother of 9)

Quick Fix for Yellow Cake Mix

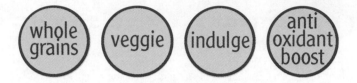

I couldn't agree with Mary-Belle S. more. Like her, many moms across the country start with a cake mix for cakes and cupcakes their kids can bring to school. Readers have requested this sneaky upgrade, which retains all the taste and texture of the original. This is a great way to respond when the school requests healthier birthday party events and bake sales.

MAKES 12 SERVINGS

3 large eggs

½ cup Orange Puree or White Bean Puree (see Make-Ahead Recipe #2, p. 44 or #9, p. 54)

⅓ cup applesauce

1 cup water

½ cup oat bran

1 box (about 18 ounces) yellow cake mix (such as Duncan Hines Moist Deluxe® Classic Yellow Cake Mix)

Preheat oven to 350 degrees and spray a cake pan with oil, then lightly dust with flour or line muffin tin with muffin cups.

In the bowl of an electric mixer, combine eggs, Orange or White Bean Puree, applesauce, water, oat bran, and cake mix. Blend at low speed for 30 seconds, then increase speed to medium for another 2 minutes. Pour batter into cake pan or muffin tins. Bake cake for 33 to 36 minutes, cupcakes for 18 to 21 minutes, both until a toothpick inserted in the center comes out clean.

PER SERVING (1 SLICE, 98G): *Calories 241; Total Fat 6.6g; Fiber 2.0g; Total Carbohydrates 41.9g; Sugars 19.0g; Protein 5.5g; Sodium 306mg; Cholesterol 53mg; Calcium 81mg.* 67% less fat, 37% less cholesterol, 93% more potassium, and 153% more fiber than traditional recipe.

Quick Fix for Chocolate Cake Mix

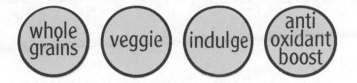

In my informal survey of moms across the country, I've found that most people use boxed cake mixes for cupcakes and cakes. Here's a way to sneak a lot more nutrition into a cake mix while maintaining its light texture and chocolaty taste.

MAKES 12 SERVINGS

3 large eggs

¾ cup **Purple Puree**
(see Make-Ahead
Recipe #1, p. 43)

1 cup water

¼ cup wheat germ

1 box (about 18 ounces)
chocolate cake mix
(such as Duncan Hines
Moist Deluxe® Classic
Cake Mix)

Preheat oven to 350 degrees and spray a cake pan with oil, then lightly dust with flour or line a muffin tin with muffin cups.

In the bowl of an electric mixer, combine eggs, Purple Puree, water, wheat germ, and cake mix. Blend at low speed for 30 seconds, then increase speed to medium for another 2 minutes. Pour batter into cake pan or muffin tins. Bake cake for 33 to 36 minutes, cupcakes for 18 to 21 minutes, both until a toothpick inserted in the center comes out clean.

PER SERVING (1 SLICE, 75G): *Calories 213; Total Fat 8.0g; Fiber 1.8g; Total Carbohydrates 33.7g; Sugars 17.3g; Protein 4.8g; Sodium 364mg; Cholesterol 52mg; Calcium 86mg. 55% less fat, 22% less cholesterol, 11% more potassium, and 41% more fiber than traditional recipe.*

Create a Sneaky Chef Healthy Bake Sale for Your Child's School

Bake sales are an important fundraising tradition. But recent concerns about childhood obesity and kids eating too much fat and sugar have caused schools nationwide to clamp down on cupcakes and ban bake sales. You can help save the cupcake by giving bake sales a better reputation. Let your school "have its cupcake and eat it, too"—so long as it builds stronger bodies.

How to do it:

■ approach the school's PTSA with the idea of an entirely Sneaky Chef bake sale

■ encourage parents to bake Sneaky Chef recipes (Brainy Brownies, Unbelievable Chocolate Chip Cookies, Santa's Sugar Cookies, Pumpkin Spice Donuts, and Quick Fixes for Yellow and Chocolate Cake Mix are especially ideal)

■ help promote the event with parents, faculty, and local press as an innovative, healthier approach that both kids and parents will love

■ get kids in on the action. Use the following handout to get them to "take the Sneaky Chef Challenge" and guess the fruit or veggie in their favorite baked good. Any time you make something into a game, kids get interested very fast

Take the Sneaky Chef Challenge!

Today you had a chance to taste some of the wonderful baked goods made for you by many helpful "sneaky chefs." You may be thinking, "What makes this bake sale sneaky?" The answer to your question is in the ingredients! Can you guess what common healthy foods were sneaked into some of the treats you ate today? Use the word box below to help you. Some words are used more than once, and some are not used at all. Have fun!

WORD BOX

spinach	carrots	blueberries	cauliflower
broccoli	zucchini	strawberries	white beans

1. I can't believe that there were _____ and _____ in my **brownies**!

2. I can't even taste the _____ that were in my **cookies**!

3. How did they get _____ and _____ into my **cupcakes**?

Fresh Cherry Slushy

Go to a movie theater and watch those slushy machines slurp around and imagine all that sugar slurping through your kids after they've begged for the blue one (raspberry) or the red one (cherry). Now you can create this movie theater favorite right at home with a fraction of the sugar and with real fresh fruit. Make sure to buy the spoon straws the kids love to drink from to make this a really authentic night out at home.

MAKES 2 SERVINGS

2 cups cold club soda

1 tablespoon sugar

2 cups frozen cherries

4 cups ice

Put club soda and sugar in a blender and blend on high. Add cherries then ice and pulse several times until the mixture is smooth enough to leave the blender on high for 1 minute. To make extra thick (this step is not essential), put the blender in the freezer for 20 to 30 minutes then blend again.

PER SERVING (388G): *Calories 115; Total Fat 0.3g; Fiber 3.0g; Total Carbohydrates 29.5g; Sugars 24.9g; Protein 1.5g; Sodium 49mg; Cholesterol 0mg; Calcium 31mg.* 47% less calories, 48% less carbs, 54% less sugars, and 37% more protein than traditional recipe.

Not the Cupcakes, Silly!

I've got quite a pair of hams for children! My six year old, Gracie, observed me buying different things at the grocery store. One day she walked in and said "I know what the Sneaky Chef is, Mom." "Oh really," I replied. She looked me in the eye and said, "See that drawing on the front, with the cook hiding a carrot behind her? I think that those recipes put secret vegetables in them." At the same time, she was eating a cupcake that I had secretly stuffed with carrots and yams. I said, "Oh, you mean, that cupcake you are eating? You think I put VEGETABLES in that?!" "Oh, no way Mom, not these. I just meant I think there are secret vegetables in that other food. Not the cupcakes, silly!" Little did she know . . .

—Meghan P., Prairie Village, KS (mother of 2)

Quick Fix for Soda Pop

Whether you call it "soda" or "pop," America's favorite beverage needs to be a lot less sweet. Rather than forbidding soda at a party or special dinner, try this trick, which significantly cuts down on the sugar content of the soda:

Mix any soda with plain seltzer —add as much plain seltzer as you can get away with. Work up to ¾ plain seltzer to ¼ soda!

Chocolate Egg Cream

My dad tells stories of sitting at the soda counter in Brooklyn and ordering an "egg cream" in those carefree times when you could order something for only a nickel (in spite of its name, there are neither eggs nor cream in an egg cream). Well, now we are more aware of the damage that the high fat and sugar content, not to mention the sky-high calorie count, can do to us. With this rescue recipe you can recreate an American tradition and slip in top-notch nutrients along the way. When kids tested both—chocolate and chocolate with Cherry Puree—they liked the sneaky one better—the other one was "too chocolaty."

MAKES 2 SERVINGS

½ cup low-fat milk

3 tablespoons chocolate syrup

¼ cup Cherry or Strawberry Puree (see Make-Ahead Recipe #7, p. 52 or #6, p. 51)

Plain seltzer

Fill glasses with one-quarter cup milk each, then add chocolate syrup, and Cherry (or Strawberry) Puree, and fill to top with seltzer. Stir well. Serve with a straw.

PER SERVING (361G): *Calories 146; Total Fat 3.2g; Fiber 1.5g; Total Carbohydrates 26.4g; Sugars 17.1g; Protein 3.7g; Sodium 173mg; Cholesterol 3mg; Calcium 117mg. 40% less calories, 57% less fat, 78% less cholesterol, 37% more protein, 50% more fiber, and 44% more potassium than traditional recipe.*

Brilliant Blondies

Normally, there is nothing redeeming nutritionally about a blondie. They are the ultimate indulgence, full of butter and caramelized brown sugar, as rich and sinful as white fudge. I enlisted the help of my baker friend, Karen, for the challenge of making a better blondie (she had helped me finalize the Brainy Brownies for my first book). She brought over her family blondie recipe and we worked from there. Days of testing and sheets and sheets of blondies later (and arm-wrestling the sticks of butter out of her hands), we succeeded in recreating the great taste and buttery richness of the caramelized flavor of the real thing. We cut half the fat and added White Bean Puree, upped the fiber, and added whole-grain nutrition with oat bran and wheat germ. Can't wait to hear what you think!

MAKES 2 DOZEN

8 tablespoons unsalted butter

1 cup packed brown sugar

1 cup **White Bean Puree (see Make-Ahead Recipe #9, p. 54)**

1 teaspoon pure vanilla extract

¼ teaspoon butterscotch flavor, optional

3 large eggs

½ teaspoon salt

¾ cup oat bran

1 cup **Flour Blend (see Make-Ahead Recipe #10, p. 56)**

¾ cup chocolate chips, white, butterscotch, or semi-sweet, optional

Preheat oven to 325 degrees. Butter or spray only the bottom, not the sides, of a 9-by-13-inch baking pan. Lightly dust with flour.

In a saucepan over medium-low heat, melt the butter and brown sugar. Remove from heat and allow mixture to cool a bit. Once cool, whisk in the White Bean Puree, vanilla, butterscotch (if using), eggs, and salt. Add the oat bran and Flour Blend and mix until just combined. Mix in the chocolate chips, if using, then pour the entire mixture into the prepared baking pan.

Bake for 30 to 33 minutes, or until a toothpick comes out clean. Allow to cool completely in pan before cutting into approximately 2" squares.

Keeps for a week in the refrigerator, covered tightly.

PER SERVING (1 BLONDIE, 40G): *Calories 123; Total Fat 4.9g; Fiber 1.8g; Total Carbohydrates 18.2g; Sugars 8.9g; Protein 3.4g; Sodium 62mg; Cholesterol 36mg; Calcium 28mg.* 32% less calories, 49% less fat, 17% less sodium, 126% more potassium, 26% less carbs, and 92% more fiber, 47% less sugars, and 82% more protein than traditional recipe.

"Benefits for everyone in the family (as the sneaky mom goes *mwahahahaha!*)"

—Shannon W., Spring Grove, IL (mother of 4)

Peanut Butter Blondies

whole grains   veggie   indulge   anti oxidant boost   protein boost

Here's another version that's sure to please. It has all the goodness of regular blondies, but with yummy peanut butter taste.

MAKES 2 DOZEN

6 tablespoons unsalted butter

1 cup packed brown sugar

1 cup Orange Puree (see Make-Ahead Recipe #2, p. 44)

¾ cup peanut butter, smooth*

2 teaspoons pure vanilla extract

2 large eggs

½ teaspoon salt

¾ cup oat bran

1 cup Flour Blend (see Make-Ahead Recipe #10, p. 56)

¾ cup semisweet chocolate chips, optional

Preheat oven to 325 degrees. Butter or spray only the bottom, not the sides, of a 9-by-13-inch baking pan. Lightly dust with flour.

In a saucepan over medium-low heat, melt the butter and brown sugar. Remove from heat and allow mixture to cool a bit. Once cool, whisk in the Orange Puree, peanut butter, vanilla, eggs, and salt. Add the oat bran and Flour Blend and mix until just combined. Mix in the chocolate chips, if using, then pour the entire mixture into the prepared baking pan.

Bake for 30 to 33 minutes, until a toothpick comes out clean. Allow to cool completely in pan before cutting into approximately 2" squares..

Keeps for a week in the refrigerator, covered tightly.

*use extra peanut butter to ice the blondies, if desired

PER SERVING (1 BLONDIE, 51G): *Calories 181; Total Fat 10.4g; Fiber 2.1g; Total Carbohydrates 19.4g; Sugars 10.4g; Protein 5.3g; Sodium 117mg; Cholesterol 36mg; Calcium 24mg.* 29% less calories, 19% less fat, 12% less sodium, 58% more potassium, 21% less carbs, and 69% more fiber, 37% less sugars, and 14% more protein than traditional recipe.

Cravin' Coffee Cake

*I'm a little embarrassed to admit that this simple coffee cake took me more than a dozen tries to perfect over the course of one weekend. I was trying to make a cherry coffee cake using the red Cherry Puree, and for some reason, the cake kept coming out green (no, there wasn't any spinach inside). When I consulted a scientist, we concluded that the acidity of the cherries combined with the baking powder caused a reaction resulting in green cake. Now, even if it were scrumptious, I couldn't let you serve something that looked like pond water, so here is an equally delicious but decidedly **not** green coffee cake with White Bean Puree! The almond extract adds a ton of flavor, by the way.*

MAKES 6–9 SERVINGS

1 cup Flour Blend (see Make-Ahead Recipe #10, p. 56)

1 teaspoon baking powder

½ teaspoon baking soda

¼ teaspoon salt

⅓ cup sugar

¼ cup canola or vegetable oil

1 large egg

¼ cup low-fat milk

1 teaspoon almond extract

¾ cup White Bean Puree (see Make-Ahead Recipe #9, p. 54)

Preheat oven to 350 degrees. Grease a 4-by-8 inch loaf pan with butter, or spray with oil. Lightly dust with flour.

In a large bowl, whisk together the Flour Blend, baking powder, baking soda, and salt. In another large bowl, whisk together the sugar, oil, egg, milk, almond extract, and White Bean Puree. Add the dry ingredients to the wet and mix just enough to moisten the dry ingredients. Transfer the batter to the prepared loaf pan. Sprinkle the optional crumb topping (next page) evenly over the top, if using, then spray the top evenly with oil. Bake for 37 to 40 minutes, or until the top is light golden brown and a toothpick inserted in the center comes out clean.

Optional Crumb Topping

2 tablespoons oat bran

1 tablespoon Flour Blend

   (see Make-Ahead Recipe #10, p. 56)

2 tablespoons packed brown sugar

½ teaspoon cinnamon

2 tablespoons cold butter, cut into small

   pieces

In a medium-size bowl, whisk together the oat bran, Flour Blend, sugar, and cinnamon. Using your fingertips, work the butter into the dry mixture evenly, forming clumps.

PER SERVING (74G): *Calories 203; Total Fat 8.2g; Fiber 3.2g; Total Carbohydrates 27.2g; Sugars 8.9g; Protein 6.1g; Sodium 211mg; Cholesterol 26mg; Calcium 86 mg.* 31% less calories, 57% less fat, 68% less cholesterol, 224% more potassium, 308% more fiber, 48% less sugars, and 56% more protein than traditional recipe.

The Sneaky Chef Celebrates

Help with the Holidays!

Dear SC,

I never thought I'd find use for a Sneaky Chef, considering my kids have grown and are now 28 and 29 years old. They are polar opposites when it comes to food—one is vegan and adamantly organic, the other a certified chef who puts taste above all else, including any health concerns. My problem is this coming Thanksgiving it'll be my turn to cook along with my daughters. I could use some pointers as to how to bridge these two disparate worlds. I want to impress my chef daughter and family with great-tasting, traditional holiday foods. At the same time, I want to respect my other daughter's wishes for healthier fare. Finally, I know holiday time is usually when we throw caution to the wind, but we're all tired of paying the price of the extra pounds at the end of the season! Please help!

— Tina R., Scarsdale, NY (mother of 2 daughters)

Perhaps no time better makes use of the family dinner table than holidays and celebrations. Loved ones actually sit and linger around meals filled with favorite dishes that become traditions, year after year. Kids run around with their friends and cousins, circling back to grab something sweet from the table. And if you're not in your dining room, you're likely being wined and dined by friends and colleagues at parties where the food is as delightful as the company around you.

So what does this translate into? Rich, sumptuous feasts that have more calories than you would normally eat in a week. It's easy to get caught up in the special occasion cheer and throw dietary caution to the winds. After all, we say to ourselves, "It's time to celebrate." Or, "I'll make up for it by dieting for a month." Beyond that, nothing will ruin your kids' (and your) happy mood faster than turning into the food police. By the time you return to your post-holiday, everyday routine, you have to face the truth: your family's eating habits are hard to get back on track.

It *is* possible to enjoy the holidays and other celebrations with good-tasting food that doesn't come with a whopping side dish of remorse. This is where the Sneaky Chef comes to the rescue. With *sneaky* recipes, you can make everything healthier and less fattening—including cake! Best of all, no one will notice that beloved indulgences are actually very virtuous.

That's just how smoothies are made!

My son (now ten years old) started making smoothies by himself a few years ago (with my supervision, of course). I was shocked and pleased to see that he added carrots and spinach. His friend said, "You put spinach and carrots in smoothies?" to which my son replied, "Yeah, it's good!" He had never questioned it . . . that's just how smoothies are made. Can you give me more easy recipes like smoothies that kids can make for us parents on special occasions? Thanks for your inspiration. I love the new recipes I can make!

—Anne J., Blacksburg, VA (mother of 2)

Valentine's Day
Red Smoothie

Every once in a while, children really want to give back—to be the caretaker for once. Here's an easy smoothie recipe that kids can make for their parents on special occasions. My girls made this for me as a breakfast-in-bed Valentine's treat last year—so easy, so red, so yummy. What a sweet way to start a day celebrating love!

MAKES 2 SERVINGS

1 cup frozen cherries, without syrup or added sweeteners (or ½ cup Cherry Puree; see Make-Ahead Recipe #7, p. 52)

1 cup frozen strawberries, without syrup or added sweeteners

½ cup pomegranate juice

2 teaspoons sugar

In the container of a blender, combine the cherries (or Cherry Puree), strawberries, pomegranate juice, and sugar, and pulse until smooth (add more juice if needed). Serve in a tall glass with a straw.

PER SERVING (299G): *Calories 110; Total Fat 0.3g; Fiber 5.0g; Total Carbohydrates 53.2g; Sugars 43.5g; Protein 2.0g; Sodium 3.0mg; Cholesterol 0mg; Calcium 33mg. 32% less calories, 88% less fat, 70% more fiber, and 84% less sugars than traditional recipe.*

Pretty Pink Popcorn Balls for Valentines

These treats are so cute that daughter Emily brought them to school for the other kids on Valentine's Day. She was the hit of the party, and they were a nice change from the heart-shaped lollipops and chocolates that the other kids shared.

MAKES 6 BALLS

6 cups *popped* popcorn

4 ounces regular marshmallows (a little less than half of a 10-ounce package)

1 teaspoon canola or vegetable oil

2 tablespoons Cherry Puree (see Make-Ahead Recipe #7, p. 52)

3 tablespoons oat bran

6 craft sticks

Place popcorn in a large bowl; set aside. In a saucepan, melt marshmallows and canola or vegetable oil over low heat. Stir in Cherry Puree and oat bran. Pour over popcorn and toss to coat. Allow to cool for 5 to 10 minutes, then spray your hands with oil and shape mixture into 6 baseball-sized balls. Re-spray hands with oil as needed.

Insert a craft stick into the end of each ball and place on waxed or parchment paper to harden. Wrap with plastic wrap and store at room temperature.

PER SERVING (1 BALL, 35G): *Calories 108; Total Fat 1.3g; Fiber 1.9g; Total Carbohydrates 24.3g; Sugars 11.6g; Protein 1.9g; Sodium 15mg; Cholesterol 0mg. 22% less calories, 72% less fat, 200% more fiber, and 30% less sugars than traditional recipe.*

Chanukah Latkes

Latkes (also known as potato pancakes) are served during Chanukah in the Jewish tradition. They are oh so delicious, especially with toppings like sour cream or apple sauce—or both mixed together. You can make the batter ahead and allow it to sit in the refrigerator for some hours (covered or the mixture turns brown) before cooking. This is not only convenient, but it's actually good for the dish because it will help hold the ingredients together. Depending on how low you want to keep the fat content, you can either pan-fry them in oil the traditional way, or oven-bake for easier (you don't have to stand at the stove) and lower-fat results.

MAKES 1 DOZEN LATKES

1½ pounds Russet potatoes
(about 2 large potatoes)

2 large eggs

3 tablespoons White Bean Puree
(see Make-Ahead Recipe #9, p. 54)

1 small onion, grated or finely chopped
(about 1 cup)

6 tablespoons whole-wheat flour

½ teaspoon salt

Freshly ground pepper, to taste

1 to 4 tablespoons canola or vegetable oil

Peel and coarsely grate the potatoes into a large bowl (add cold water to the bowl if you are not cooking the latkes immediately—this will prevent the potatoes from turning brown). You can refrigerate the grated potatoes in water for up to a day, if necessary.

When ready to cook, drain potatoes in a colander and press down with your hand to squeeze out as much water as possible. While the potatoes are draining, beat the eggs with the White Bean Puree in a large mixing bowl. Add the onion to the same bowl. Stir in the grated potatoes, flour, salt, and a few grinds of pepper. Mix well.

Below are two ways to cook the latkes. The oven method is a lower-fat time-saver, and the result is nearly as good as pan-frying.

Serve with plain yogurt (or low-fat sour cream) and/or applesauce.

Oven-baked method:

Preheat the oven to 400 degrees. Rub a baking sheet with 1 tablespoon canola or vegetable oil. Form ¼-cup-sized scoops of the potato mixture into flat patties and place them on the prepared baking sheet. Spray the tops of the latkes generously with oil and bake for 15 minutes. Remove the pan from the oven, flip the patties, spray the other side with oil, and bake for another 15 minutes.

Pan-fry method:

Heat 2 tablespoons of oil over medium-high heat in a large (10- or 12-inch) nonstick skillet. Reduce the temperature to medium if the oil starts to smoke. Working in batches of 4 to 6 latkes, scoop about ¼ cup of the potato mixture into the hot skillet and flatten gently with the back of a spatula. Reduce heat to medium and cook until one side is golden brown, about 5 minutes. Turn over and brown the other side. Repeat with the next batch of 4 latkes, adding more oil to the pan as needed. Place the cooked latkes on a plate lined with paper towels to blot away excess oil.

PER SERVING (1 BAKED LATKE, 80G): *Calories 79; Total Fat 1.0g; Fiber 2.1g; Total Carbohydrates 14.8g; Sugars 0.8g; Protein 3.3g; Sodium 112mg; Cholesterol 35mg.* 59% less fat, 63% less cholesterol, 92% more fiber, 50% more potassium, and 37% less sugars than traditional recipe.

Shirley Temple for Special Occasions

veggie · anti oxidant boost

This popular "kiddie cocktail" is a nonalcoholic drink named after the famous child actress of the forties, Shirley Temple. Kids often like to order a "Shirley Temple" in a restaurant on special occasions so they can feel like grown-ups sipping a cocktail. It is traditionally made with red syrup, ginger ale, and a maraschino cherry; you can upgrade the nutritional value of this cocktail and still let kids have all the fun.

MAKES 4 KID COCKTAILS

1 cup pomegranate juice

1 teaspoon sugar

2 cups plain seltzer or club soda

1 cup ginger ale or lemon-lime soda

Fresh or maraschino cherries

Combine pomegranate juice and sugar in a saucepan over medium-high heat. Bring to a boil, then reduce to a simmer, stirring occasionally, until the sugar dissolves and the mixture thickens to a more syrupy consistency and reduces to about ½ cup—about 10 minutes. Remove from the heat and allow to cool before mixing with remaining ingredients. Serve in tall glasses over ice and garnish each cocktail with a cherry.

Time-saving note: If you're in a rush, just use pomegranate juice without cooking it.

PER SERVING (187G): *Calories 69; Total Fat 0.0g; Fiber 0.1g; Total Carbohydrates 17.5g; Sugars 15.2g; Protein 0.1g; Sodium 31mg; Cholesterol 0mg; Calcium 9mg.* 39% less calories, 85% less fat, 84% less carbs, and 87% less sugars than traditional recipe.

Christmas Morning Smoothie

On Christmas morning, what kid wouldn't be thrilled to come downstairs to a hill of presents and find beside the Christmas tree a red and green-layered smoothie—not for Santa Claus, but for them. Never mind that it's cold outside and you were thinking a steaming bowl of oatmeal might have been a better choice; the kids are going to get a real kick out of this nutrient-packed breakfast. Plus, the good fat and fiber in the avocado will keep them energized all morning long. Hey, it's hard work unwrapping all those gifts!

MAKES 2 SERVINGS

1 frozen banana

½ ripe avocado

1 teaspoon green
    decorating sugar

2 cups skim milk

1 cup frozen strawberries,
    without syrup or
    added sweeteners

In the container of a blender, combine the banana, avocado, green sugar, and 1 cup of the milk. Blend on high until smooth. Pour into two tall glasses until each is half full. Add strawberries and remaining 1 cup of milk to the same blender and blend on high until smooth. Pour the red smoothie on top of the green smoothies (do *not* stir or mix). You should have two distinct layers—green and red—in each glass. Top with a squirt of whipped cream and a sprinkle of green sugar. Serve with a straw.

PER SERVING (467G): *Calories 280; Total Fat 8.3g; Fiber 7.2g; Total Carbohydrates 43.6g; Sugars 14.7g; Protein 11.9g; Sodium 151mg; Cholesterol 4mg; Calcium 378mg.*

Roasted Squash Soup
for the Holidays

Cutting a fresh squash can be daunting if you don't have a lot of upper body strength. If you bake it as you would a whole potato, it's easy to slice open after it's cooked. This creamy fat-free soup is a great first course to start a holiday dinner. The recipe evolved over time as I started adding apples and cinnamon for a hint of sweet and tang. It can be as homey or elegant as you wish. Using a handheld blender to puree all the ingredients makes this really simple to create.

MAKES 6 TO 8 SERVINGS

1 large butternut squash

1 red onion, quartered

4 cups vegetable broth, ideally low-sodium

¼ teaspoon cinnamon

1 apple, peeled and quartered

1 cup Orange Puree (see Make-Ahead Recipe #2, p. 44)

½ cup evaporated skim milk

Salt to taste

Optional Garnish: ¼ cup toasted, shelled pumpkin seeds

Preheat oven to 375 degrees.

Rinse the whole squash, prick with fork (as you would a baked potato), place on a baking sheet with the onion, and bake for 45 minutes.

Remove squash and onion from oven. Set the onion aside while you cut open the squash and scoop the flesh from the skin. Discard the seeds. Place the squash flesh, onion, broth, cinnamon, salt, apple, and Orange Puree in a large soup pot. Bring to a simmer and cook for 15 to 20 minutes. Use an immersion blender to puree the soup to a smooth consistency.

Alternatively, you can puree the soup in batches using a blender.

Stir in the evaporated milk, if using, and serve. Top with toasted pumpkin seeds, if using.

PER SERVING (389G): *Calories 180; Total Fat 1.4g; Fiber 5.4g; Total Carbohydrates 39.0g; Sugars 12.2g; Protein 5.3g; Sodium 605mg; Cholesterol 2mg; Calcium 157mg.* 35% less calories, 91% less fat, and 91% less cholesterol than traditional recipe.

Garlic Mashed Potatoes for Thanksgiving

The "Mighty Mashed Potatoes" from my Sneaky Chef book for men were so popular that I decided to use a similar recipe for holiday entertaining. There are so many heavy foods at Thanksgiving; these mashed potatoes make for a wonderfully lighter version of the traditional.

Serve them with a ladle of Sneaky Gravy, and you have a complete protein even without the turkey. Perfect for vegetarians who have to give up so much during the season.

MAKES 4 SERVINGS

2 pounds Yukon gold or russet potatoes (about 4 medium-sized potatoes), peeled and quartered

2 to 3 heads garlic

½ cup White Puree (see Make-Ahead Recipe #4, p. 48)

½ cup low-fat plain yogurt*

2 tablespoons extra-virgin olive oil

½ teaspoon salt

Freshly ground pepper, to taste

"Greek" style yogurt works best with this recipe

Preheat oven to 350 degrees.

Place the potatoes in a large pot of cold, salted water and bring to a boil. Lower the heat, cover, and simmer for 25 to 35 minutes, until the potatoes are completely tender.

Meanwhile, wrap the garlic heads in foil and roast them in the oven for 30 minutes. Remove the garlic from the oven and squeeze the garlic flesh out of the skins.

Drain the potatoes, then return them to the pot. Add the roasted garlic flesh, White Puree, yogurt, olive oil, salt, and pepper. Mash with a potato masher until well combined. Add a bit more yogurt if needed. Serve immediately, or keep the mashed potatoes hot on the stovetop in a metal bowl set over simmering water.

Serve with a ladle of Sneaky Gravy, on page 209.

PER SERVING (232G): *Calories 247; Total Fat 7.6g; Fiber 3.6g; Total Carbohydrates 40.7g; Sugars 4.2g; Protein 6.5g; Sodium 328mg; Cholesterol 1mg; Calcium 122mg.* 33% less calories, 71% less fat, 98% less cholesterol, 39% more protein, and 36% less sodium than traditional recipe.

Sneaky Gravy

IMHO—online speak for "in my humble opinion"—there's nothing sexy about gravy. In fact, it's my least favorite part of Thanksgiving dinner since it traditionally needs to be made at the last minute from pan drippings as guests are just arriving at your door. You can cheat a little and make this gravy with a good quality packaged chicken broth, or do it the traditional way from the turkey itself. Either way, the Lentil Puree adds a depth of hearty flavor as well as a great dose of fiber that will help rid the body of all that unhealthy fat that's just accepted as an unavoidable part of this holiday meal.

MAKES ABOUT 3 CUPS GRAVY

2 tablespoons butter or pan drippings (from chicken or turkey)

1½ tablespoons whole-wheat flour

2 cups chicken broth, ideally low-sodium

1½ teaspoons Worcestershire sauce (or Gravy Master®)

½ cup Lentil Puree (see Make-Ahead Recipe #5, p. 50)

Salt and freshly ground pepper, to taste

Optional Extra Boost: ½ onion, minced or pureed

Heat the butter or pan drippings over medium heat in a sauté pan. Add the onion (if using) and cook until lightly browned, about 10 minutes. Whisk in the flour, the broth, Worcestershire sauce (or Gravy Master®) and Lentil Puree. Cook for about 5 minutes or until thickened. Season with salt and pepper to taste.

Serve hot with mashed potatoes and turkey.

PER SERVING (¼ CUP, 193G): *Calories 41; Total Fat 2.2g; Fiber 1.3g; Total Carbohydrates 3.4g; Sugars 0.3g; Protein 2g; Sodium 161, Cholesterol 5mg.* 54% less calories, 72% less fat, 70% less cholesterol, 15% less carbs, an astronomical 25 times more fiber, 32% more potassium, 29% more protein, and 21% less sugars than traditional recipe.

Sammy's Pumpkin Spice Donuts (or Muffins)

Why wait for the annual trip to the pumpkin patch to enjoy a hot spiced donut, when you can easily make them anytime at home? This recipe has more fiber, pure vegetables, and whole grain, plus it is low in fat. Get yourself an inexpensive donut pan at the housewares store and convert all your muffin recipes to seemingly more decadent donuts!

MAKES 6 MUFFINS OR 12 DONUTS

1¼ cups Flour Blend (see Make-Ahead
    Recipe #10, p. 56)

2 teaspoons baking powder

½ teaspoon salt

2½ teaspoons pumpkin pie spice
    (or equal parts cinnamon, ground ginger,
    and nutmeg)

2 large eggs

3 tablespoons walnut, canola,
    or vegetable oil

½ cup packed brown sugar

Handwritten note: 1 ½ T cinnamon / ½ t Cardamom / ½ t ginger / ¼ t Nutmeg

Handwritten note: Coconut Oil melted

Handwritten note: Coconut Sugar ¼ / Honey ¼

6 tablespoons Orange Puree
    (see Make-Ahead Recipe #2, p. 44)

½ cup pumpkin puree

Handwritten note: Try 1¼ c Oat Bran / ½ c. almond flour packed / no orange puree / ½ c. Milk or yogurt Kefir

Preheat oven to 350 degrees and spray a mini-bundt (or donut) pan with oil. For cupcakes, line a muffin tin with paper liners.

In a large bowl, whisk together the Flour Blend, baking powder, salt, and pumpkin pie spice. In another large bowl, whisk together the eggs, oil, sugar, Orange Puree, pumpkin puree, and vanilla until well combined. Fold the wet ingredients into the dry and mix until the flour is just moistened. Don't overmix. Pour into donut molds or fill muffin cups almost to the top. Spray tops of donuts or muffins with oil before baking.

For donuts: Bake 14 to 16 minutes or until the tops spring back when pressed lightly. Loosen the edges with a knife and turn the donuts out over a plate. Allow to cool and then decorate as desired.

For muffins: Bake 22 to 24 minutes or until a toothpick inserted in the center comes out clean. Turn the muffins out of the tins to cool. Dust tops with powdered sugar or decorate as desired.

PER SERVING (1 MUFFIN OR 2 DONUTS, 80G):
Calories 239; Total Fat 8.7g; Fiber 2.6g; Total Carbohydrates 36.8g; Sugars 18.5g; Protein 5.0g; Sodium 342mg; Cholesterol 35mg. 31% less cholesterol, 192% more fiber, and 210% more potassium than traditional recipe.

Gingerbread Men for the Holidays

Kids love to participate in holiday baking and decorating. This is a holiday classic, but oh-so-much healthier, and it's even more fun to make than the original. As we've heard from many readers, the kids get an added kick out of sneaking vegetable purees on themselves and their friends and then pretending they don't know about it. Decorate to your heart's content. These cookies freeze well for up to 3 months.

MAKES ABOUT 4 DOZEN

3 cups Flour Blend (see Make-Ahead Recipe #10, p. 56)

½ **teaspoon** *each* **baking soda and salt**

2 teaspoons ground ginger

1 teaspoon cinnamon

½ **cup canola or vegetable oil**

½ **cup packed brown sugar**

⅓ **cup molasses**

½ **cup Orange Puree (see Make-Ahead Recipe #2, p. 44)**

In a large mixing bowl, whisk together the Flour Blend, baking soda, salt, ground ginger, and cinnamon, and set aside.

In another mixing bowl, whisk the oil, sugar, molasses, and Orange Puree. Add the dry ingredients to the wet and mix well (using your hands) until a moist dough forms. Add a tablespoon or two of water if needed. Remove dough from bowl and shape into a ball. Wrap in parchment paper or plastic wrap and refrigerate for at least 1 hour.

Preheat oven to 350 degrees. Lightly grease a cookie sheet or line it with parchment paper.

When ready to bake the cookies, remove the dough from the refrigerator and roll it out on a lightly floured surface (or between two sheets of parchment paper) to about ⅛-inch. Cut out the dough using gingerbread-shaped cookie cutters. Place cookies on prepared baking sheet and bake for 13 to 15 minutes or until golden brown. Let cool before decorating.

Store cookies in airtight container at room temperature.

PER SERVING (1 MAN, 16G): *Calories 62; Total Fat 2.6g; Fiber 0.8g; Total Carbohydrates 9.2g; Sugars 3.6g; Protein 1.2g; Sodium 40mg; Cholesterol 0mg.* 200% more fiber, 26% more protein, and 24% less sugars than traditional recipe.

Holiday Green Bean Casserole

Classically, this is a Campbell's soup recipe, but we've upgraded it a bit with the addition of extra veggies and whole grains while retaining its great taste and ease of preparation. Here are a few of the things I did to make this Thanksgiving standard a lot better for you:

1. *Used frozen (or fresh) green beans, not canned.*

2. *Used low-sodium, low-fat cream of mushroom soup (like "Healthy Request")—one-quarter the fat; half the calories.*

3. *Slipped in some extra veggies and fiber (White Puree and oat bran).*

4. *Added this optional extra: fresh mushrooms.*

MAKES 8 SERVINGS

1 can (10¾ ounces) cream of mushroom soup (ideally Campbell's "Healthy Request")

½ cup low-fat milk

1 teaspoon low-sodium soy sauce

½ cup **White Puree (see Make-Ahead Recipe #4, p. 48)**

2 tablespoons oat bran

One 16- to 20-ounce bag fresh or frozen green beans

1 cup canned fried onions

Optional Extra Boost: **1 cup sliced fresh mushrooms**

Preheat oven to 350 degrees and spray a 2-quart casserole dish with oil.

In the prepared casserole dish, mix the soup, milk, soy sauce, White Puree, oat bran, green beans, and sliced mushrooms, if using. Bake for 25 minutes. Remove from oven, stir, and top with the fried onions. Bake for another 5 minutes.

PER SERVING (132G): *Calories 97; Total Fat 3.9g; Fiber 2.5g; Total Carbohydrates 12.0g; Sugars 2.4g; Protein 2.5g; Sodium 252mg; Cholesterol 0mg; Calcium 49mg.* 40% less calories, 57% less fat, 100% less cholesterol, 30% less carbs, and 53% less sodium than traditional recipe.

Soufflé Surprise for Thanksgiving

So many readers have enjoyed the Orange Puree "straight up" that I'm using it as the basis for this classic sweet potato soufflé. Although I've never made a soufflé in my life (the fancy French name is enough to scare me away), this is actually one of the easiest recipes in the book. If you have the time to make the crumb topping, it's truly wonderful, but also delicious without it. Serve hot out of the oven when it's at its height of puffiness. (Souffles always deflate as they cool.)

MAKES 8 SERVINGS

2 large eggs

4 egg whites

2 tablespoons unsalted butter, softened

2 cups Orange Puree (see Make-Ahead Recipe #2, p. 44)

¼ cup sugar

1 cup evaporated skim milk

1 teaspoon pure vanilla extract

1 tablespoon whole-wheat flour

1 teaspoon salt

Optional Toppings: **8 marshmallows or pie crust topping, below**

Optional Pie Crust Topping

3 tablespoons Flour Blend (see Make-Ahead Recipe #10, p. 56)

3 tablespoons Ground Walnuts (see Make-Ahead Recipe #13, p. 60)

3 tablespoons oat bran

1½ tablespoons sugar

¼ teaspoon cinnamon

1½ tablespoons walnut, almond, canola or vegetable oil

Preheat oven to 350 degrees. Spray 8 ramekins or a 2-quart casserole dish with oil.

In the bowl of an electric mixer, beat eggs and egg whites on high for about a minute. Add in the butter, Orange Puree, sugar, evaporated milk, vanilla, flour, and salt. Pour mixture into the prepared baking dish or individual ramekins (don't fill all the way to the top, since the soufflés will puff up).

If using the optional pie crust topping, bake for 15 minutes, then remove from oven and sprinkle evenly. Return to oven for another 15 minutes.

Alternatively, if using marshmallows as topping, bake for 25 minutes, then place marshmallows on top and return to the oven for about 5 minutes or until marshmallows are lightly browned and melted.

PER SERVING, NO TOPPING (131G): *Calories 140; Total Fat 4.3g; Fiber 1.8g; Total Carbohydrates 18.8g; Sugars 12.8g; Protein 6.6g; Sodium 410mg; Cholesterol 61mg; Calcium 121mg.* 21% less fat, 30% more potassium, 21% less carbs, and 150% more protein than traditional recipe.

"The Orange Puree is a hit all on its own. Sprinkle a little cinnamon on it and call it dessert! YUMMY!"

—Stephanie J., Mooresville, NC (mother of 2)

Santa's Sugar Cookies

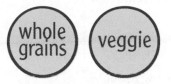

Perfect for cookie-cutter shapes, this holiday classic provides a blank slate for decorating in endlessly creative ways. Beyond holiday time, the versatility of the basic sugar cookie makes them a big hit at school bake sales. Make a few extra batches and freeze in plastic bags so they're always on hand. When your kids come home and want a mid-afternoon treat, hand them these instead of packaged cookies.

MAKES ABOUT 4 DOZEN COOKIES

8 tablespoons unsalted butter, softened

2 cups Flour Blend (see Make-Ahead Recipe #10, p. 56)

½ teaspoon salt

½ cup sugar, plus more to sprinkle

½ cup White Bean Puree (see Make-Ahead Recipe #9, p. 54)

2 teaspoons pure vanilla extract

1 large egg

In a large mixing bowl, whisk together the flour and salt and set aside.

In the bowl of an electric mixer, beat butter and sugar until creamy. Beat in White Bean Puree, vanilla, and egg. Slowly add the Flour Blend and salt, a little at a time, and mix on low speed just until all the flour is incorporated. Remove dough from bowl and shape into a ball. Wrap in parchment paper or plastic wrap and refrigerate for at least 1 hour.

Preheat oven to 350 degrees. Lightly grease a cookie sheet or line it with parchment paper.

When ready to bake the cookies, remove the dough from the refrigerator and roll it out on a lightly floured surface (or between two sheets of parchment paper) to about ⅛ inch thick. Cut out the dough using shaped cookie cutters. Place cookies on prepared baking sheet and sprinkle with sugar (omit sugar is you are planning to decorate the cookies). Bake for 14 to 16 minutes or until golden brown. Let cool before decorating.

Store cookies in airtight container for up to 3 days, or freeze them in a plastic bag for up to 3 months.

PER SERVING (1 COOKIE, 15G): *Calories 49; Total Fat 2.3g; Fiber 0.7g; Total Carbohydrates 6.5g; Sugars 2.1g; Protein 1.3g; Sodium 26mg; Cholesterol 9mg; Calcium 6mg.* 24% less calories, 36% less fat, 59% less sodium, 157% more potassium, 17% less carbs, and 271% more fiber, 36% less sugars, and 78% more protein than traditional recipe.

Candy Cane Biscotti

I love biscotti because they are among the lowest-fat cookies around (that's what makes them so deliciously crunchy). Trying to shape these crunchy cookies into a bent candy cane shape for the Christmas tree can be tricky, but whatever shape you end up with will be just as delicious. Let the kids in on decorating these treats, like dipping the ends in melted white chocolate or adding green and red sprinkles or broken pieces of candy cane.

MAKES ABOUT 18 BISCOTTI

¼ cup canola or vegetable oil

½ cup sugar

¾ cup **Purple Puree (see Make-Ahead Recipe #1, p. 43)**

⅛ teaspoon peppermint extract, optional

1 large egg

½ teaspoon salt

2 cups plus 1 tablespoon Flour Blend (see Make-Ahead Recipe #10, p. 56)

3 tablespoons unsweetened cocoa

Optional Decorations: ½ cup white chocolate chips and ½ cup green and red sprinkles (or 3 candy canes, broken into small pieces)

Preheat oven to 350 degrees. Line a baking sheet with parchment paper (or spray with oil).

In a large bowl, whisk together the oil, sugar, Purple Puree, peppermint extract (if using), egg, and salt. In another large bowl, whisk together the Flour Blend and cocoa. Add the dry ingredients to the wet and mix just enough to moisten the dry ingredients.

Place the dough on the prepared baking sheet and use your fingers to form it into a log approximately 4 inches wide by 9 inches long. Spray the top of the log with oil and bake for 20 minutes, remove from the oven, and let cool for 5 minutes.

Place the log on a cutting board. Using a serrated knife, cut the log into diagonal slices about ½ inch wide. Place the slices back on the baking sheet, spray with oil, and bake for another 30 minutes. Allow biscotti to cool before decorating.

To decorate:

If using candy cane option, using a rolling pin, gently crush the candy canes (in a sealed plastic bag) into coarsely crushed pieces. Pour crushed candy onto a plate. If using sprinkles, pour sprinkles onto a plate.

Place white chocolate chips in a microwave-safe bowl and microwave on high until melted, checking (and stirring) them every 15 seconds to prevent burning. Immediately dip about ⅓ of the biscotti into the melted white chocolate, let the excess chocolate drip off, and then sprinkle with candy cane pieces or sprinkles. Allow to cool on parchment or wax paper (refrigerate for a few minutes to cool more quickly, if desired).

PER SERVING (1 BISCOTTI, 38G): *Calories 36; Total Fat 4.0g; Fiber 1.9g; Total Carbohydrates 16.7g; Sugars 6.5g; Protein 2.8g; Sodium 72mg; Cholesterol 11mg.* 75% less calories, 58% less cholesterol, 86% more potassium, 36% less carbs, 108% more fiber, and 57% less sugars than traditional recipe.

Bountiful Pumpkin Pie

This is one of the easiest pies to make (especially if you start with pure canned pumpkin). It is naturally very forgiving—when you lower the fat and sugar content, it still remains rich and creamy with that distinctive pumpkin flavor. And it's a piece of cake sneaking Orange Puree into it. Use your favorite pie crust or the sneaky pie crust below.

MAKES 8 SERVINGS

⅓ block (about 5 ounces) firm tofu

1 can (15 ounces) pure pumpkin puree

½ cup **Orange Puree (see Make-Ahead Recipe #2, p. 44)**

3 large eggs

½ cup sugar

1 teaspoon pure vanilla extract

½ cup low-fat vanilla yogurt

2½ teaspoons pumpkin pie spice

½ teaspoon salt

1 tablespoon cornstarch

One store-bought pie crust or Holiday Pie Crust (next page)

Preheat oven to 425 degrees.

Place the tofu and pumpkin puree in the bowl of a food processor or blender and puree on high until very smooth. If your food processor or blender is large enough, add the Orange Puree, eggs, sugar, vanilla, yogurt, spice, salt, and cornstarch and process for a few more seconds. Alternatively, transfer tofu mixture to a large bowl and whisk in the Orange Puree, eggs, sugar, vanilla, yogurt, spice, salt, and cornstarch.

Pour the pumpkin mixture over the prepared crust and bake for 15 minutes. Reduce heat to 350 degrees, and cook for an additional 45 to 55 minutes. Let cool for a few minutes, then refrigerate at least 3 hours before serving.

PER SERVING (1 SLICE, 158G): *Calories 249; Total Fat 10.4g; Fiber 2.5g; Total Carbohydrates 33.8g; Sugars 21.2g; Protein 7.5g; Sodium 267mg; Cholesterol 80mg.* 45% less cholesterol, 16% less carbs, 382% more fiber, 18% more potassium, and 44% less sodium than traditional recipe.

Holiday Pie Crust

MAKES 1 PIE CRUST

6 tablespoons Flour Blend (see Make-Ahead Recipe #10, p. 56)

6 tablespoons Ground Walnuts (see Make-Ahead Recipe #13, p. 60)

6 tablespoons oat bran

¼ teaspoon salt

3 tablespoons sugar

½ teaspoon cinnamon

3 tablespoons walnut, almond, canola or vegetable oil

Preheat the oven to 350 degrees. Spray a 9-inch pie pan with oil.

In a medium-size bowl, combine the Flour Blend, ground walnuts, oat bran, salt, sugar, and cinnamon. Mix in the oil. Press the mixture into the prepared pie pan, prick it a few times with a fork, and bake for 14 to 16 minutes, until golden brown.

> **PER SERVING (1 WHOLE CRUST, 190G):** *Calories 950; Total Fat 64.7g; Fiber 12.2g; Total Carbohydrates 95.9g; Sugars 39.2g; Protein 17.6g; Sodium 586mg; Cholesterol 0mg. 150% less cholesterol, 138% more fiber, 91% more potassium, 32% less sodium, and 26% more protein than traditional recipe.*

Sneaky Chef Light

Kids' Favorites Made Lighter, Please!

Dear Missy,

I have loved The Sneaky Chef and have gotten my kids (and my husband) to eat a slew of foods they don't even know they are eating. And even when they know I made something from The Sneaky Chef, they love it anyway. My daughter repeatedly asks for your "magic meatballs." I think those were the first things I tried, and no one could believe they had vegetables and wheat germ. I have one daughter who is very picky. She is so fussy we can't get her to eat anything. She loves desserts (and what kid doesn't). Believe it or not she loves making Sneaky Chef desserts and has even gotten used to the idea of putting the vegetables in to puree herself. As long as she can't see them in the final product, it doesn't bother her to eat them.

My other daughter is a bit more challenging. She is gaining weight more rapidly than we would like, and I don't want to fight with her about what she is eating. Our doctor suggested that she not gain more weight as she grows and that she eat only one dessert a week: a near impossibility in our lives with dinners out and birthday and school parties galore. It just seems impossible to keep healthy (and in this instance lower-calorie and lower-fat) eating a priority.

Since she loves your recipes, I am just wishing that you could now figure out how to make the Sneaky Chef recipes a bit lighter. I don't want to single her out and deprive her of the goodies that the *other kids get to eat. Plus our entire family could benefit from eating lighter (who couldn't?). Maybe that's too much to ask, but is there any chance you could adapt some of the great Sneaky Chef recipes or find new ones that would be low-cal as well? Boy I hope you can help with this one.*

—(name withheld by request)

I was amazed at just how many parents contacted me to say that even though they believed they were doing everything right, their children were beginning to put on weight too rapidly for their height. If they said anything about it to their kids, they were either met with denial, "I am not," or with a hurt look. If they made suggestions about diet or exercise, they were met with resistance. For those parents who tried to research the matter, they were confronted with contradictory advice. "Don't say anything because you'll make them self-conscious." "Don't ignore it or the problem will just get worse."

The fact is there *is* reason for alarm. The statistics on childhood obesity in this country are disturbing. One third of all kids under 18 are overweight and 17 percent are considered to be obese.

Many factors contribute to this troubling trend. Children live in a far more sedentary environment than they used to and they spend more time indoors in front of computer and television screens. Research shows that when kids eat at home, they eat less because they are supervised. However, these days the family dinner appears to be becoming a quaint relic. Many parents work long hours, and children have busy after-school schedules that make home-cooked meals scarce—and when they happen, quick. Children (as well as adults) aren't reaching for fresh fruits and vegetables; instead they're opting for fast, prepackaged foods that are high in calories and preservatives. (Metabolically, many foods are now "obesogenic," which means they are tailor-made to fatten you up and contain things like high-fructose corn syrup and transfats—which our bodies store up rather than use for energy). Plus, they're buying giant-sized juices, sugary coffee drinks, sodas, and even calorie-packed flavored waters, and as a consequence are gulping the bulk of their calories.

BRILLIANT
BLONDIES

Sneaky ingredients:
White beans,
wheat germ,
whole wheat

ICY HOT
CHOCOLATE
AND
MONKEY BARS

*Sneaky ingredients
(Monkey Bars):*
Yams, carrots, oats,
whole wheat, and
wheat germ
*Sneaky ingredients
(Icy Hot Chocolate):*
Yogurt and
wheat germ

VALENTINES PARTY: RED SMOOTHIE AND PINK POPCORN BALLS

Sneaky ingredients: Cherries, strawberries, pomegranate, oat bran

THANKSGIVING: GREEN BEAN CASSEROLE, MASHED POTATOES, GRAVY, PUMPKIN PIE, SOUFFLÉ SURPRISE

Sneaky ingredients (green bean casserole): Oat bran, cauliflower, zucchini

Sneaky ingredients (mashed potatoes): Yogurt, cauliflower, zucchini

Sneaky ingredients (pie): Tofu, yams, carrots, oat bran, walnuts

Sneaky ingredients (souffle): Carrots, yams

CHRISTMAS MORNING SMOOTHIE, GINGERBREAD MEN, SUGAR COOKIES, & CANDY CANE BISCOTTI

Sneaky ingredients (smoothie): Avocado, strawberries

Sneaky ingredients (gingerbread men): Wheat germ, carrots, yams, whole wheat

Sneaky ingredients (biscotti): Spinach, blueberries, wheat germ, whole wheat

Sneaky ingredients (sugar cookies): White beans, wheat germ, whole wheat

ROASTED SQUASH SOUP FOR THE HOLIDAYS

Sneaky ingredients: Carrots, yams, apples, onions, vegetable broth

LIGHT BRAINY BROWNIES

Sneaky ingredients: Spinach, blueberries, oat bran, wheat germ, whole wheat

GLUTEN-FREE PIZZA

Sneaky ingredients: Chickpeas, carrots, yams, cauliflower and zucchini

GLUTEN-FREE CHOCOLATE CHIP COOKIES

Sneaky ingredients: White beans, whole wheat, wheat germ

GLUTEN-FREE CHICKEN TENDERS

Sneaky ingredients: Carrots, yams

That's the bad news. Here's the good news. There is a solution: serve them the food they love, but make sure it is a healthier, less fattening, lower-calorie version. When parents try to persuade kids to make weight-conscious choices, it is often counterproductive. According to *US News and World Report,* when parents joke or cajole, their kids "are more likely to engage in binge eating, which leads to weight gain over time. And when parents harp on children's body weight, kids are also likely to become preoccupied with achieving thinness."

The Sneaky Chef methods allow parents to approach the issue without *making* it an issue.

And there are things that you can do that go beyond sneaking:

1. **Doctors who specialize in obesity in children say that the best scenario is to let kids "grow into their weight" instead of lowering their weight. In other words, unlike adults, kids are growing taller every day. If they can manage to stay at the same weight** while **they're growing, they will automatically trim down.**

2. **Bring back the habit of eating at home. Not only does it let parents supervise what their kids are eating, but it provides a foundation for the family.**

3. **Use smaller plates and smaller portions, and avoid the "family style" method of serving. If huge platters are plunked in front of you, it'll be easy to put more on your plate without even thinking about it.**

4. **If you make any item into the "forbidden fruit," they'll want it all the more. Instead, give them not-so-great foods in modest amounts periodically so their desire doesn't grow out of hand.**

5. **Teach your children to listen to their bodies and hunger cues. The key is to eat when they're hungry and stop eating when they're not. Often (like many adults), they're eating more because they're bored, sad, depressed, or need comfort than because they're truly hungry.**

6. **Make sure that they feel satisfied once they've eaten. Nothing encourages overeating more than the feeling of deprivation. Sneaky Chef recipes are packed with ingredients like complex carbs and proteins and are designed to keep you** feeling fuller longer.

7. **Most importantly, you have to be modeling the right behavior. When the whole family decides to improve its diet, the kids follow suit.**

Light Brainy Brownies

These brownies achieved as nice a chocolaty richness as the original *Brainy Brownies*, with less than half the fat. You'll notice the addition of plain yogurt and extra *Purple Puree*, which took the place of some of the higher-fat butter and chocolate.

MAKES ABOUT 30 BROWNIES

3 tablespoons unsalted butter

½ cup semi-sweet chocolate chips

2 large eggs

¼ cup vanilla yogurt

2 teaspoons pure vanilla extract

½ cup sugar

¾ **cup Purple Puree (see Make-Ahead Recipe #1, p. 43)**

¼ teaspoon cinnamon

1 teaspoon instant coffee powder

¼ cup unsweetened cocoa powder

¼ teaspoon salt

½ **cup Flour Blend (see Make-Ahead Recipe #10, p. 56)**

¼ cup oat bran

½ teaspoon baking powder

Powdered sugar, for dusting

Preheat oven to 350 degrees.

Butter or spray, then lightly flour, the bottom of a 9-inch square baking pan.

Melt the butter and chocolate chips in a double boiler or metal bowl over simmering water (or in a microwave, checking every 15 seconds). Remove from heat and allow mixture to cool a bit. Meanwhile, in another bowl, whisk together the eggs, yogurt, vanilla, sugar, and Purple Puree. Combine the purple egg mixture with the cooled chocolate mixture.

In a mixing bowl, whisk together cinnamon, coffee, cocoa, salt, Flour Blend, oat bran, and baking powder. Add this to the chocolate mixture and blend thoroughly. Pour the entire mixture into the baking pan.

Bake for 36 to 40 minutes, until a toothpick comes out clean. Allow to cool completely in the pan before cutting the brownies using a plastic or butter knife. Dust with powdered sugar, if desired.

Keeps for a week in the refrigerator, covered tightly.

PER SERVING (1 BROWNIES, 19G): *Calories 53; Total Fat 2.6g; Fiber 0.6g; Total Carbohydrates 7.5g; Sugars 5.3g; Protein 1.1g; Sodium 32mg; Cholesterol 17mg.* Compared to Sneaky Chef Original Brainy Brownies recipe 17% less calories, 32% less fat, 7% less cholesterol, 3% less carbs, 3% more fiber, 4% more potassium, 5% more protein, and 6% less sugars.

Light Mac 'n' Cheese

This lighter version of my original Masterful Mac 'n' Cheese replaces half the quantity of cheese with evaporated skim milk and White or Orange Puree. It has a satisfying and creamy texture, and kids prefer that it's made on the stovetop (like the boxed versions) rather than oven-baked.

MAKES 4 SERVINGS

White Version:

1½ cups evaporated skim milk

¼ cup White Puree (see Make-Ahead Recipe #4, p. 48)

4 ounces reduced-fat light-colored cheese (like white cheddar)

2 tablespoons grated Parmesan cheese

1 tablespoon unsalted butter

½ teaspoon mustard (ideally honey mustard; don't use spicy mustard)

4 cups cooked elbows or other small pasta shape (about ½ pound dry)

Mix everything except pasta together in pot over low heat. Add pasta and stir.

Yellow Version:

Follow recipe above, substituting reduced-fat yellow cheddar for white cheddar, and add 4 teaspoons Orange Puree.

PER SERVING (237G): *Calories 338; Total Fat 6.6g; Fiber 4.3g; Total Carbohydrates 49.8g; Sugars 12.6g; Protein 22.9g; Sodium 331mg; Cholesterol 19mg; Calcium 449mg.* 44% less calories, 76% less fat, 78% less cholesterol, 62% less sodium, 23% less carbs, and 80% more fiber than traditional recipe.

Couldn't Get It Fast Enough

I have very picky eaters at my house. I started with the mac 'n' cheese recipe, hoping no one would find out what I did. My oldest son (who is the pickiest) had two big helpings and my youngest (nine months old) was getting mad that we weren't feeding him fast enough. You have allowed moms like me, who stress proper nutrition for children who refuse to eat well, to sleep better at night.

—Mindi B., Keller, TX (mother of 3)

Light Chocolate Chip Cookies

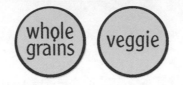

I was very pleased with the way these lower-fat chocolate chip cookies turned out. While I wasn't able to reduce the sugar content (which was already low in the original recipe), I did manage to successfully replace half the butter with more White Bean Puree. Another good trick here is to use mini chocolate chips so you get more chips per cookie for fewer calories. Making these cookies smaller lets kids have two for the price of one.

MAKES ABOUT 4 DOZEN COOKIES

1 cup Flour Blend (see Make-Ahead
   Recipe #10, p. 56)

½ teaspoon each baking soda and salt

¼ cup oat bran

4 tablespoons unsalted butter, softened

¼ cup packed brown sugar

¼ cup sugar

2 egg yolks

2 teaspoons pure vanilla extract

½ cup White Bean Puree (see Make-Ahead
   Recipe #9, p. 54)

½ cup plain yogurt

½ cup semisweet chocolate chips
   (ideally "mini" chocolate chips)

Preheat oven to 350 degrees.

In a large bowl, whisk together Flour Blend, baking soda, salt, and oat bran. Set aside.

In the bowl of an electric mixer, beat butter and both sugars until creamy. Beat in egg yolks, vanilla, White Bean Puree, and yogurt. Add dry ingredients to wet and mix on low speed. Stir in chocolate chips. Make small cookies by dropping rounded teaspoonfuls, spaced about 1 inch apart, onto nonstick or parchment-lined baking sheets. Spray tops of cookies lightly with oil and flatten with the back of a spatula.

Bake for 14 to 16 minutes or until golden brown. Let cool on a metal rack.

Store cookies in airtight container for up to 3 days, or freeze them in a plastic bag for up to 3 months.

PER SERVING (1 COOKIE, 14G): *Calories 44; Total Fat 1.9g; Fiber 0.6g; Total Carbohydrates 6.4g; Sugars 3.3g; Protein 1.1g; Sodium 39mg; Cholesterol 10mg; Calcium 10mg.* 33% less calories, 49% less fat, 62% more potassium, 47% more fiber, 29% more protein, and 37% less sugar than traditional recipe.

Sneaky Tip:

Double or triple this recipe and save some of the batter rolled in plastic wrap in the freezer for homemade "slice and bake" cookies anytime.

Quick Fixes for Peanut Butter

whole grains · veggie · anti oxidant boost · protein boost · low carb · low sugar

Peanut butter is not only a favorite among most kids (I love it too!), but it's a pretty good food nutritionally. It is high in "good" fat, but at nine grams of fat per tablespoon, it can pack on the pounds in both kids and adults. That's why I put this recipe in the "Light" section of the book— the additions below will not only add a good quantity of nutrients, but lower the caloric density.

Tip: Let peanut butter soften at room temperature before mixing in the sneaky ingredients below.

Mix one of the following boosters into 2 tablespoons of peanut butter. Stir until well combined (I find it easiest to do this on a plate and mix with the back of a fork) and make your sandwich as usual.

• 1 tablespoon White Bean Puree (see Make-Ahead Recipe #9, p. 54)

• 1 tablespoon Orange Puree (see Make-Ahead Recipe #2, p. 44)

• 1 tablespoon wheat germ (this is easier to get away with when using "crunchy" peanut butter)

*Try to choose peanut butter that doesn't have high-fructose corn syrup or any hydrogenated oil. These days, you can even get low-fat versions.

Sneaky Tip:

Label alert! Even if jar of peanut butter claims "no trans fats," flip it over and read the ingredients, looking for partially hydrogenated oils. If it's listed, it's in there (although in small enough amounts that the label can still say no trans fats), and every little bit adds up.

Light Sugar Cookies

The regular sugar cookies (Santa's Sugar Cookies, page 217) are already slimmed down, but surprisingly, I was able to remove even more butter by adding extra White Bean Puree. In side-by-side testing against the original, kids barely noticed any difference. This recipe features 35 percent less fat.

MAKES ABOUT 4 DOZEN COOKIES

2 cups Flour Blend
(see Make-Ahead
Recipe #10, p. 56)

½ teaspoon salt

4 tablespoons unsalted
butter, softened

⅓ cup sugar

¾ cup White Bean Puree
(see Make-Ahead
Recipe #9, p. 54)

2 teaspoons pure vanilla
extract

1 large egg

In a large mixing bowl, whisk together the Flour Blend and salt and set aside.

In the bowl of an electric mixer, beat butter and sugar until creamy. Beat in White Bean Puree, vanilla, and egg. Slowly add the flour mixture, a little at a time, and mix on low speed just until all the flour is incorporated. Remove dough from bowl and shape into a ball. Wrap in parchment paper or plastic wrap and refrigerate for at least 1 hour.

Preheat oven to 350 degrees. Lightly grease a cookie sheet or line it with parchment paper.

When ready to bake the cookies, remove the dough from the refrigerator and roll it out on a lightly floured surface (or between two sheets of parchment paper) to about ⅛ inch thick. Cut out the dough using shaped cookie cutters. Place cookies on prepared baking sheet and sprinkle with sugar (omit sugar is you are planning to decorate the cookies). Bake for 14 to 16 minutes or until golden brown. Let cool before decorating.

Store cookies in airtight container for up to 3 days, or freeze them in a plastic bag for up to 3 months.

PER SERVING (1 COOKIE, 13G): *Calories 41; Total Fat 1.3g; Fiber 0.8g; Total Carbohydrates 6.2g; Sugars 1.4g; Protein 1.4g; Sodium 26mg; Cholesterol 6.0mg; Calcium 7mg.* 35% less calories, 62% less fat, 58% less sodium, 225% more potassium, 16% less carbs, and 374% more fiber, 54% less sugars, and 107% more protein than traditional recipe.

Light Green Goddess Dressing

Before the world was introduced to ranch dressing, "Green Goddess" was one of the most popular salad dressings in the country. To achieve the best of both worlds, this recipe combines fresh Green Puree with a low-fat ranch dressing as a base.

MAKES ABOUT ½ CUP

2 tablespoons low-fat
  ranch dressing

Juice of whole lime

1 tablespoon red wine
  or apple cider vinegar

2 tablespoons Green
  Puree (see Make-Ahead
  Recipe #3, p. 46)

Salt and freshly ground
  pepper, to taste

In a medium-size bowl, whisk together the ranch dressing, lime juice, vinegar, and Green Puree. Season with salt and pepper. Cover and store in the refrigerator for up to 3 days.

PER SERVING (2T, 60G): *Calories 46.5; Total Fat 2.6g; Fiber 1.2g; Total Carbohydrates 6.4g; Sugars 1.2g; Protein 0.6g; Sodium 142mg; Cholesterol 3mg.* 75% less calories, 83% less fat, 83% less cholesterol, 33% less carbs, 416% more fiber, 57% less sodium, and 50% less sugars than traditional recipe.

CHAPTER SEVEN

Sneaky Chef for Food Allergies

"As a nurse practitioner, I think this book is a work of art and health! Question for you: my son is sensitive to dairy and soy. Is there a replacement that you know of to use in your recipes?"

—Jyotika V., Silver Spring, MD (mother of 1)

Parents whose children have allergies carry a special burden. Not only do they have to be alert to what their children eat at home, they have to try to protect them when they go to a birthday party, a group picnic, or a school outing. An allergic reaction takes place when a person encounters something the body thinks is a toxin—either by breathing it (pollen, for example) or by eating it (foods, such as peanuts). The body believes it is being attacked and launches a series of offenses that lead to symptoms like stomachaches, sneezing, itching, hives, or swelling of the throat. Usually, the symptoms are no more than troublesome, but sometimes they are downright dangerous. At least 15,000 people visit the emergency room because of severe reactions to a food allergy; 150 people die from reactions every year.

No one knows exactly why there's been such a dramatic rise in food allergies among children in the last ten years, but it is interesting to note that the beginning of the epidemic coincides with the arrival of genetically modified (GM) foods. Basically, these foods are grown to make their own insecticides. We cannot wash the insecticide off; they are *in* the fabric of the food, not *on* it. Scary and strange, isn't it?

Another theory is that, paradoxically, we are *too* clean—clean water, vaccines, and antibiotics have eliminated most of the toxins we used to live with, and thus adapted to. Studies support the fact that kids who grow up on farms, where they're exposed to dirt, germs, and animals, don't often develop allergies.

Schools are becoming more alert to food allergy issues and are learning to change lunchroom and classroom snack policies, and even parents of kids without allergies are paying attention to what they serve a group of children. Even so, many kids are reluctant to stand out from the crowd and say, "I can't eat that," when everyone around them is digging in, which means Mom and Dad have to be the watchdogs. Many readers have told me that they feel like they're constantly on high alert because so much is at stake.

I wrote this chapter because I feel there is an unaddressed need in cookbooks for tasty meals for kids who are deprived of the old standbys that we all had as kids—peanut butter and jelly sandwiches (peanuts), Spaghetti-Os (wheat), ice cream (milk), pudding (eggs), and other treats. Even if there are substitutes available, they don't come close to tasting like the real thing. Parents have complained to me that they have to travel far and wide just to find a store that stocks allergy-friendly foods that actually have flavor. Usually, the foods their kids *can* eat without worry simply have to be endured, and are never enjoyed. The following recipes offer a friendly, accessible way to work around the offending allergy.

Nancy's Celiac Success Story

This is from Nancy Shedrofsky, who contributed gluten-free recipes to this chapter:

My son was diagnosed with celiac disease in 2004 at age 13. It was overwhelming at first trying to figure out what foods he could and couldn't have. It seemed the only place to shop was Whole Foods Market or other natural-food stores. Grocery stores were filled with packaged foods, and all of the things we used to buy now had to be scrutinized carefully for hidden ingredients that included gluten.

The chicken broth I cooked with and the barbecue sauce my kids enjoyed? Off limits because of wheat starch. Cheerios and other breakfast cereals he was used to? No good—they contain malt. Even the mini can of potato chips I used to put in his lunch contained wheat.

Most of the gluten-free (GF) foods had to be ordered online, but they were expensive and he didn't like the gritty consistency or taste of the breads, cookies, and baked goods. So, I started baking everything for him—it simply tasted better. Plus, my other two children, who don't have celiac disease, could eat them as well.

Thankfully, I'm an accomplished cook and baker myself and have been able to make gluten-free dinners for the whole family. I substitute gluten-free breadcrumbs, soy sauce, and other ingredients, and I have been able to successfully make meals that everyone likes.

I'm happy that you're addressing the concerns of families like mine by making GF recipes that are actually tasty and healthy. So many food manufacturers are making foods that may be GF, but are otherwise not very healthy. I'm excited that you've asked me to help you sneak some of your famous spinach and blueberry puree into GF brownies! Plus, I'm especially hopeful that you'll be helping me to come up with GF pancakes that are tasty and healthy, because we've yet to find one in all these years of tasting and searching!

Gluten-Free Flour Blend

MAKES ABOUT 3 CUPS

---

2 cups rice flour (ideally
   brown rice flour)

²/₃ cup potato starch
   (not potato flour)

¹/₃ cup tapioca flour
   (or tapioca starch)

1 teaspoon xanthan gum

Combine all ingredients in a bowl. This blend can be stored in a sealed, labeled plastic bag in the refrigerator for up to 3 months.

Note: most of the gluten-free ingredients in this chapter can be found at Whole Foods Market or on Amazon.com.

PER SERVING (3 CUPS, 462G): *Calories 1727; Total Fat 4.9g; Fiber 14.3g; Total Carbohydrates 386.9g; Sugars 4.1g; Protein 26.2g; Sodium 63mg; Cholesterol 0mg; Calcium 101mg.*

GF Flour Blend is used in the following recipes:

Gluten-Free Pancakes

Gluten-Free Chocolate Chip Cookies

Gluten-Free Brownies

Gluten-Free Peanut Butter Cookies

Gluten-Free Better Breading

MAKES 2 ½ CUPS BREADING

½ cup almonds, slivered and blanched (omit if allergic)

1½ cups Rice Krispies®

½ cup cornmeal

2 tablespoons Parmesan cheese

Freshly ground pepper, to taste

Pulse the almonds in a food processor. Don't let the food processor run continually or you will end up with nut butter. Pour the almond meal into a large plastic bag. Add the Rice Krispies to the bag and gently crush with a rolling pin. Add the cornmeal, Parmesan cheese, and pepper to the bag. Close and shake the bag. Refrigerate for up to 2 weeks.

PER SERVING (2.5 CUPS, 167G): *Calories 959; Total Fat 54.9g; Fiber 15.6g; Total Carbohydrates 140.9g; Sugars 7.3g; Protein 28.0g; Sodium 1744mg, Cholesterol 8mg.*

GF Better Breading is used in the following recipe:

Gluten-Free Chicken Tenders

Gluten-Free Pancakes

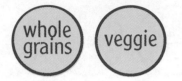

My friend Nancy S. came over and worked with me on this and other gluten-free recipes to follow. Her GF son hadn't had pancakes in years because he had never found one he liked. This GF recipe gave her son back his pancakes, and even his non-GF brother loved them, meaning that mom could make just one batch for the family. The key to the texture, it turned out, is to cook the pancakes longer over lower heat.

MAKES ABOUT 18 PANCAKES

¾ cups GF Flour Blend (see p. 248)

2 teaspoons baking powder

½ teaspoon salt

¼ cup Ground Almonds (see Make-Ahead
   Recipe #11, p. 58) (omit if allergic)

¼ cup unsweetened applesauce
   (or grated fresh apple)

¼ cup vanilla yogurt

1 teaspoon pure vanilla extract

2 tablespoons low-fat milk

1 large egg

2 tablespoons honey or pure maple syrup

Optional Extra Boost: ¼ cup chocolate chips
   or ¼ cup fresh or frozen blueberries

Sneaky Tip:

Be sure to buy gluten-free versions of all the ingredients listed in the following recipes (even chocolate chips and other ingredients can be suspect for gluten—read labels carefully for safety).

Mix together GF Flour Blend, baking powder, salt, and ground almonds (optional). Set aside, if using immediately. (To store for later use, triple the dry ingredients and keep in a sealed, labeled plastic bag in the refrigerator. You'll have instant GF pancake mix anytime you want it.)

In another bowl, whisk together the applesauce, yogurt, vanilla, milk, egg, and honey (or maple syrup) and optional blueberries or chocolate chips, if desired. (If using frozen berries, don't thaw them before adding; this will prevent bleeding.) Add the wet ingredients to the dry ones until just blended. If the batter is too thick, add a little more milk.

Butter or spray a large skillet over medium-low heat. Test the pan to see if it's hot enough by tossing a few drops of water in—it should sizzle. The skillet will grow hotter over time, so turn it down to low if it starts to smoke.

Drop tablespoons or small ladles of batter onto the skillet in batches. When bubbles begin to set around the edges of the pancake and the skillet-side is golden (peek under), gently flip them over. Continue to cook 2 to 3 minutes or until the pancake is set.

Serve stacked high, drizzled with a little warm maple syrup.

PER SERVING (1 PANCAKE, 22G): *Calories 48; Total Fat 1.2g; Fiber 0.4g; Total Carbohydrates 8.3g; Sugars 2.3g; Protein 1.2g; Sodium 112mg; Cholesterol 12mg.*

Gluten-Free Chocolate Chip Cookies

My gluten-free friend and personal fitness trainer, Larysa, came for lunch recently, and I served her these GF cookies. She hadn't eaten a good chocolate chip cookie since she went off gluten and wheat years ago. As she reached for her third cookie, she said, "Yum! The store-bought GF cookies taste sandy and gritty, but these are sooo good!" Every time we train together, I restock her freezer with a fresh batch.

MAKES ABOUT 4 DOZEN

1 cup GF Flour Blend (see p. 248)

½ teaspoon baking soda

½ teaspoon salt

8 tablespoons unsalted butter, softened (substitute a trans-fat-free non-dairy margarine if allergic to dairy)

¼ cup sugar

¼ cup packed brown sugar

2 egg yolks

1 teaspoon pure vanilla extract

¼ cup White Bean Puree (see Make-Ahead Recipe #9, p. 54)

½ cup semisweet chocolate chips (use non-dairy chocolate chips if allergic to dairy)

Preheat oven to 350 degrees.

In a large bowl, whisk together GF Flour Blend, baking soda, and salt. Set aside.

In the bowl of an electric mixer, beat butter and both sugars until creamy. Beat in egg yolks, vanilla, and White Bean Puree. Add dry ingredients and mix on low speed. Stir in chocolate chips. Make small cookies by dropping rounded teaspoonfuls, spaced about 1 inch apart, onto nonstick or parchment-lined baking sheets. Spray tops of cookies lightly with oil and flatten with the back of a spatula.

Bake for 16 to 18 minutes or until golden brown. Let cool on a metal rack.

Store cookies in airtight container for up to 3 days, or freeze them in a plastic bag for up to 3 months.

PER SERVING (1 COOKIE, 11G): *Calories 50; Total Fat 2.7g; Fiber 0.3g; Total Carbohydrates 6.1g; Sugars 3.1g; Protein 0.5g; Sodium 39mg, Cholesterol 12mg.*

Gluten-Free Pizza Crust

As I've said before, the true taste test for a good GF product is whether non-GF kids like it too. That also solves another problem for Mom, since she can finally make one recipe for the entire family and not single out her allergic child with a separate recipe. My daughter Sammy, who fortunately is not allergic to gluten, proclaimed "Oh, yeah, that's delicious" when I asked her to give this a try—and that was even before I added the sauce and cheese!

MAKES ONE MEDIUM PIZZA CRUST

1 tablespoon olive oil

½ cup **Chickpea Puree (see Make-Ahead Recipe #8, p. 53)**

1 large egg

½ teaspoon each oregano, onion powder and garlic powder

½ cup grated Parmesan cheese (substitute rice or soy cheese if allergic to dairy)

½ cup GF flour (such as garbanzo flour or rice flour)

Preheat oven to 375 degrees and brush the olive oil in the center of a baking sheet.

In a mixing bowl, combine Chickpea Puree with the egg, oregano, onion powder, garlic powder, and Parmesan cheese. Add the GF flour and mix until well blended. Lightly oil your hands, then remove the mixture from the bowl and shape into a large ball.

Place the dough on the oiled cookie sheet and, using the palm of your hand, press it into an imperfect, rustic flat circle or oval shape. Don't cover the entire baking sheet. Spray the top side of the dough generously with oil.

Bake for 15 minutes, then remove from oven and save (wrapped in foil) in the refrigerator for use within 3 days, or proceed to make pizza immediately (opposite page).

PER SERVING (1 WHOLE CRUST, 317G): *Calories 846; Total Fat 35.3g; Fiber 7.4g; Total Carbohydrates 94.2g; Sugars 1.3g; Protein 36.4g; Sodium 1775mg; Cholesterol 255mg.*

Gluten-Free Pizza

MAKES 4 SERVINGS

One GF Pizza Crust
   (see opposite page)

¾ cup pizza sauce

¼ **cup Orange or White**
   Puree (see Make-Ahead
   Recipe #2, p. 44 or #4,
   p. 48)

1 cup low-fat mozzarella
   cheese (substitute rice
   or soy cheese if allergic
   to dairy)

Optional Extra Boost:

   sliced mushrooms,
   onions, sweet peppers,
   or artichoke hearts

Preheat oven to 400 degrees and preheat a pizza stone, if using one, or spray a baking sheet with oil.

Place GF Pizza Crust on the prepared baking sheet. In a mixing bowl, combine pizza sauce with Orange or White Purees. Spread sauce mixture across the pizza dough, then top with the cheese and any optional toppings. Bake for 10 to 15 minutes until bubbly and lightly browned. Allow to cool a few minutes, then cut into triangles and serve.

PER SERVING (1 SLICE, 169G): *Calories 333; Total Fat 14.8g; Fiber 6.3g; Total Carbohydrates 35.0g; Sugars 5.2g; Protein 15.9g; Sodium 971mg; Cholesterol 74mg; Calcium 322mg.*

Gluten-Free Brownies

You don't have to have a gluten allergy to love these healthy brownies. They are rich and luscious without most of the worry. They're safe both from high sugar content and from wheat sensitivities that affect so many people. Allergic kids no longer have to feel deprived when home-baked goodies are served.

MAKES ABOUT 16 BROWNIES

6 tablespoons unsalted butter

¾ cup semisweet chocolate chips

2 large eggs

½ cup sugar

2 teaspoons pure vanilla extract

½ cup **Purple Puree (see Make-Ahead**
   Recipe #1, p. 43)

1 tablespoon cornstarch

1 tablespoon unsweetened cocoa powder

¼ teaspoon cinnamon

1 teaspoon instant coffee powder

½ cup **GF Flour Blend (see p. 248)**

¼ teaspoon salt

Optional Extra Boost: 1 cup chopped walnuts

Powdered sugar, for dusting

Preheat oven to 350 degrees. Butter or spray, then lightly flour the bottom of a 8-inch or 9-inch square baking pan.

Melt the butter and chocolate chips together in a double boiler or metal bowl over simmering water (or in a microwave, checking every 15 seconds). Remove from heat and allow mixture to cool a bit. Meanwhile, in another bowl, whisk together the eggs, sugar, Purple Puree, and vanilla. Combine this purple egg mixture with the cooled chocolate mixture.

In a mixing bowl, whisk together the cornstarch, cocoa powder, cinnamon, coffee, GF Flour Blend, and salt. Add this to the chocolate mixture and blend thoroughly. Mix in the chopped walnuts, if using, then pour the entire mixture into the baking pan.

Bake for 32 to 35 minutes, or until a toothpick comes out clean. Allow to cool completely in pan before cutting the brownies using a plastic or butter knife. Dust with powdered sugar, if desired.

Keeps for a week in the refrigerator, covered tightly.

PER SERVING (1 BROWNIE, 41G): *Calories 134; Total Fat 7.4g; Fiber 1.0g; Total Carbohydrates 16.7g; Sugars 11.4g; Protein 1.6g; Sodium 79mg; Cholesterol 37mg.*

Gluten-Free Peanut Butter Cookies

Gluten-free eaters complain that their cookies are oftentimes gritty, weird tasting, not particularly healthy (not low-fat or low sugar), and horribly expensive. Since the only major manufacturing concern is the flour, I simply substituted my Flour Blend and then went on to learn the chemistry of a whole new way of baking. Just as in other sneaky recipes, peanut butter provides the perfect disguise for similarly sweet, similarly colored Orange Puree, which allowed me to cut down on a good amount of sugar. The peanut butter (of course, this isn't for kids who can't eat peanuts) is the fat, so there's no need for butter. Adding a few chocolate chips to the middle of the cookie also adds extra kid appeal.

MAKES 2 DOZEN COOKIES

½ cup smooth peanut butter

½ cup **Orange Puree (see Make-Ahead Recipe #2, p. 44)**

½ cup sugar, plus a little extra for dusting

1 large egg

1 teaspoon pure vanilla extract

6 tablespoons **GF Flour Blend (see p. 248)**

1 teaspoon baking soda

¼ cup semisweet chocolate chips or

   ¼ cup favorite jam, optional

Preheat oven to 350 degrees and spray a baking sheet with cooking spray (or line with parchment paper).

In a large mixing bowl, whisk together peanut butter, Orange Puree, sugar, egg, and vanilla. Add in Flour Blend and baking soda and mix just until combined. Drop rounded tablespoonfuls spaced about 1 inch apart onto nonstick or parchment-lined baking sheets. Gently press your thumb into the center of each ball to make an indent. Fill the indent with a few chocolate chips or ½ teaspoon of jam, if using (if not, simply flatten cookies with the back of a fork).

Bake 11 to 13 minutes, or until golden brown.

PER SERVING (1 COOKIE, 19G): *Calories 63; Total Fat 3.0g; Fiber 0.6g; Total Carbohydrates 7.9g; Sugars 4.9g; Protein 1.8g; Sodium 83mg; Cholesterol 8mg.*

Gluten-Free Chicken Tenders

My gluten-free friends and readers have two words to describe packaged GF chicken nuggets and tenders: mushy and weird! Since I have never had to eat this way myself, I decided to do a little taste-testing among some of the packaged GF chicken available in my markets. I have to admit, I couldn't even finish a single nugget! They were, indeed, strange tasting and the texture was just plain off. Here is the sneaky version of a GF tender, proclaimed by my GF tasters as "crispy and delicious."

MAKES 4 TO 6 SERVINGS

1 pound boneless, skinless chicken tenders (or boneless, skinless chicken breasts, cut into strips)

½ cup cornstarch

2 large eggs

¼ cup Orange Puree (see Make-Ahead Recipe #2, p. 44)

2 cups GF Better Breading (see p. 249)

½ cup grated Parmesan cheese

Olive oil for pan-frying method

Salt and freshly ground pepper, to taste

Season chicken tenders with salt. Place cornstarch in a shallow dish or on a plate. Beat eggs with Orange Puree in a shallow bowl and place next to the cornstarch. In a third shallow dish or on a paper plate, combine the GF Better Breading with the Parmesan cheese.

Dredge each piece of chicken in the cornstarch, shaking off excess, then the egg mixture, and then the GF Better Breading mixture. Press the breading evenly onto both sides of the chicken. Put on waxed or parchment paper and store in the refrigerator for cooking the next day, or proceed to cook immediately.

Pan-fry method:

Heat 2 tablespoons oil in a large skillet over moderately high heat until hot but not smoking. Add a few strips at a time, pan-frying on one side until the crumbs look golden, about 2 to 3 minutes. Watch for burning, and turn down heat if necessary. With tongs, turn the pieces over and lightly brown the second side until golden, about 3 minutes. Reduce the heat to low and continue heating chicken until cooked through, about another 10 minutes. Blot cooked tenders on paper towels to remove excess oil.

Oven-bake method (not as brown and crisp, but easier):

Preheat oven to 400 degrees.

Place breaded tenders on a lightly sprayed cookie sheet and bake for 10 to 12 minutes. Turn chicken tenders over once with tongs, then return to oven for another 10 to 12 minutes until cooked through.

PER SERVING (153G): *Calories 405; Total Fat 12.5g; Fiber 4.7g; Total Carbohydrates 44.5g; Sugars 1.5g; Protein 28.8g; Sodium 260mg; Cholesterol 121mg; Calcium 145mg.*

"My son is allergic to nuts. Can you redo your chocolate chip cookie recipe without the ground almonds? Thanks!"

— *Melissa M., Oro Valley, AZ (mother of 2)*

Eggless and Nutless Chocolate Chip Cookies

My adorable vegetarian brother Larry, (aka "Uncle Ninny") helped create this egg-and-nut-free version of the ever-popular Unbelievable Chocolate Chip Cookies from the first Sneaky Chef. *Even non-allergic kids like my daughter proclaimed these "better than normal cookies!" You can hardly beat that.*

MAKES ABOUT 4 DOZEN COOKIES

1 tablespoon arrowroot powder

1 tablespoon cornstarch

2 tablespoons water

1 cup Flour Blend (see Make-Ahead Recipe #10, p. 56)

½ teaspoon baking soda

½ teaspoon salt

¼ cup oat bran

8 tablespoons unsalted butter (substitute a trans-fat-free non-dairy margarine if allergic to dairy)

¼ cup sugar

¼ cup packed brown sugar

1 teaspoon pure vanilla extract

¼ cup White Bean Puree (see Make-Ahead Recipe #9, p. 54)

½ cup semisweet chocolate chips

Preheat oven to 350 degrees. Remove butter from refrigerator to let soften.

Dissolve arrowroot powder and cornstarch in the water; set aside.

In a large bowl, whisk together Flour Blend, baking soda, salt, and oat bran. Set aside.

In the bowl of an electric mixer, beat butter and both sugars until creamy. Add in arrowroot-cornstarch mixture, vanilla, and White Bean Puree. Add dry ingredients and mix on low speed. Stir in chocolate chips. Drop rounded teaspoonfuls of batter, spaced 1 inch apart, onto a nonstick baking sheet (or line the sheet with parchment paper). Bake for 15 to 17 minutes or until golden brown. Let cool on a metal rack.

Store cookies in airtight container at room temperature.

PER SERVING (1 COOKIE, 11G): *Calories 47; Total Fat 2.6g; Fiber 0.5g; Total Carbohydrates 6.1g; Sugars 3.1g; Protein 0.7g; Sodium 38mg; Cholesterol 5.0mg.* 14% less calories, 15% less fat, 38% less cholesterol, 40% more fiber, 40% more potassium, and 25% less sugars than traditional recipe.

Eggless Pancakes

True vegetarians swear by this recipe that was generously submitted by Jim F. in Sedona, Arizona. I am most appreciative because I know that getting any rise out of a pancake without eggs is a true feat of nature.

MAKES ABOUT 18 PANCAKES

1 cup Flour Blend (see Make-Ahead
  Recipe #10, p. 56)

½ teaspoon baking soda

¼ teaspoon salt

1 tablespoon canola or vegetable oil

1 tablespoon sugar

1 cup low-fat buttermilk*

1 teaspoon pure vanilla extract

Optional Extra Boosts: ½ cup fresh or frozen
  blueberries or chocolate chips

(*if you don't have buttermilk on hand, make your own by mixing 1 cup low-fat milk with 1 tablespoon lemon juice; let stand 5 minutes)

Mix together Flour Blend, baking soda, and salt. Set aside, if using immediately. (To store for later use, triple the dry ingredients and keep in a sealed, labeled plastic bag. You'll have instant pancake mix anytime you want it.)

In another bowl, whisk together the oil, sugar, buttermilk, and vanilla. Add the wet ingredients to the dry ones until just blended. If the batter is too thick, add a little more buttermilk. Add the optional blueberries or chocolate chips, if desired, and mix lightly. (If using frozen berries, don't thaw them before adding; this will prevent bleeding.)

Butter or spray a large skillet over medium heat. Test the pan to see if it's hot enough by tossing a few drops of water in—it should sizzle.

The skillet will grow hotter over time, so turn it down if it starts to smoke.

Drop tablespoons or small ladles of batter onto the skillet in batches. When bubbles begin to set around the edges of the pancake and the skillet side is golden (peek under), gently flip them over. Continue to cook 2 to 3 minutes or until the pancake is set.

Serve stacked high drizzled with warm maple syrup.

Cinnamon-Apple Pancake Variation:

Follow the instructions for Eggless Pancakes above, adding ½ teaspoon of cinnamon and substituting a peeled, chopped apple for the chocolate chips or blueberries. For smoother texture, grate the apple before adding it to the batter. Serve with a dusting of cinnamon sugar.

PER SERVING (1 PANCAKE, 22G): *Calories 39; Total Fat 1.2g; Fiber 0.6g; Total Carbohydrates 5.9g; Sugars 1.4g; Protein 1.5g; Sodium 81mg; Cholesterol 0mg.* 18% less calories, 33% less fat, 12% less cholesterol, 363% more potassium, 15% less carbs, and 227% more fiber, 30% less sugars, and 48% more protein than traditional recipe.

"My daughter cannot tolerate dairy or eggs. How can I make the breakfast cookies (or granola bars) with substitutes for the dairy and egg?"

—Angela D., Bronx, NY (mother of 1)

Egg-Free, Dairy-Free, Gluten-Free Granola Bars

Many parents of GF kids complain that their kids eat too many marshmallow treats (because it's one of the gluten-free treats available in the market), and they certainly wouldn't give them to the children for breakfast due to their high sugar content. These GF bars are a cross between a granola bar and Rice Krispie treat.

MAKES 2 DOZEN BARS

2 cups cornflakes, crushed to about 1 cup

½ cup **Ground Almonds (see Make-Ahead Recipe #11, p. 58)**

2 cups crispy brown rice cereal (or Rice Krispies®)

½ teaspoon cinnamon

½ teaspoon salt

¼ cup canola or vegetable oil

½ cup honey

1 teaspoon pure vanilla extract

¼ cup semisweet chocolate chips (optional; omit if allergic to dairy)

Optional Extra Boost: ¼ cup raisins or dried blueberries

Preheat oven to 350 degrees. Line a 9-inch square or 11-by-7 inch baking pan completely with parchment paper or foil and butter the foil (or spray with oil).

In a medium bowl, combine crushed cornflakes, Ground Almonds, rice cereal, cinnamon, and salt. Mix in the canola or vegetable oil, honey, vanilla extract, chocolate chips, and dried fruit, if using. Mix well, then pour into the prepared baking pan. Press down with palm of hand, evenly distributing the mixture into the corners of the dish, and bake for 15 to 18 minutes. Check occasionally to prevent burning.

Remove from the oven and, using the foil to help you, lift the entire bar out of pan. Place on a flat surface and, while still warm, cut into small bars.

Store in an airtight container or freeze in plastic bags.

PER SERVING (1 BAR, 16G): *Calories 79; Total Fat 3.8g; Fiber 0.4g; Total Carbohydrates 11.4g; Sugars 7.3g; Protein .8g; Sodium 88mg; Cholesterol 0mg.*

Sneaky Tip:

Measure the oil first, then the honey. This way the honey won't stick and will slide right out of the measuring cup.

Egg-Free, Dairy-Free, Gluten-Free Grits Sticks

Many of my GF families requested a substitute for the carbs that kids love in the morning—toast, cereal, bagels. These sticks are hearty whole-grain replacements. Plus the grain and beans in this dish form a complete protein. You can easily make it ahead and freeze, then toast when ready.

MAKES 6 SERVINGS

2 cups water

6 tablespoons grits

¼ teaspoon salt

¼ cup **White Bean Puree (see Make-Ahead Recipe #9, p. 54)**

¼ cup grated Parmesan cheese, optional (omit if allergic to dairy)

Spray an 11-by-7-inch or 9-inch square baking pan with oil. Place a piece of parchment paper on the bottom.

Stir the water, grits, and salt into a saucepan and bring to a boil. Reduce heat to low, cover, and cook for 15 minutes. Stir in the White Bean Puree and cheese, if using. Immediately transfer the grits to the prepared baking pan, cover the pan with foil, and refrigerate until firm, at least 1 hour and as long as 24 hours.

Preheat oven to 425 degrees and spray a baking sheet with oil.

Cut the chilled grits into French fry–sized sticks or wedges and place them on the prepared baking sheet. Spray the top generously with oil and bake for 10 minutes. Flip the sticks, spray with more oil, and bake for another 10 minutes or until golden brown. Serve hot.

PER SERVING (279G): *Calories 74; Total Fat 1.4g; Fiber 1.0g; Total Carbohydrates 11.8g; Sugars 0.1g; Protein 3.7g; Sodium 163mg; Cholesterol 3mg; Calcium 61mg.*

Eggless Banana Pancakes from Boxed Mix

Give your favorite boxed pancake mix a delicious homemade taste with the simple addition of some sweet superfruits, veggies, and whole grains. In an instant, you've upgraded this universal packaged food into an excellent product.

MAKES ABOUT 18 PANCAKES

1 tablespoon canola or vegetable oil

1 large banana, mashed

¾ cup low-fat milk (substitute rice milk if allergic to dairy)

¼ cup Orange Puree (see Make-Ahead Recipe #2, p. 44)

1 cup boxed pancake mix

¼ cup wheat germ

Preheat griddle to medium-high and spray with oil.

In a medium bowl, whisk together the oil, banana, milk, and Orange Puree. In another large bowl, whisk the boxed pancake mix and wheat germ. Add the wet ingredients to the dry ones until just blended. If batter is too thick, add a touch more milk.

Test the pan by tossing in a few drops of water; it will sizzle when it's hot enough. The skillet will grow hotter over time, so turn down the heat if the pan starts to smoke.

Drop medium-size ladles of batter onto the skillet in batches. When bubbles begin to set around the edges and the skillet side of each pancake is golden (peek underneath), gently flip them over.

Continue to cook 2 to 3 minutes or until the pancake is fully set.

Serve stacked high, drizzled with a little warm maple syrup.

PER SERVING (1 PANCAKE, 30G): *Calories 52; Total Fat 1.4g; Fiber .7g; Total Carbohydrates 8.7g; Sugars 1.6g; Protein 1.6g; Sodium 94mg; Cholesterol 2mg.* 20% less fat, 80% less cholesterol, 56% more potassium, and 72% more fiber than traditional recipe.

Need an Egg Substitute
for Brainy Brownies

I am just starting to be sneaky with my picky 3-year-old and husband. My question is about the egg substitution. My daughter is allergic to eggs, so I use a soy-based egg substitute for muffins. Unfortunately, it doesn't work for brownies—I'm wondering if you can recommend a substitute when wet eggs are required (such as for pancakes and brownies, etc.). I've had a little luck with thinned yogurt, but the result ends up gummy. Thanks!

—Robin R., San Rafael, CA (mother of 2)

Eggless Brainy Brownies

I received numerous requests for baked goods from parents of children with egg allergies. Not everyone has access to the egg replacers at natural foods stores; plus, they can be expensive and the results are often inconsistent. I keep a stash of these in the freezer for the times when my vegan brother, Larry, comes to visit. Plus, according to my daughter Emily, there's a side benefit:

"My mom is always nervous about me eating brownie batter because of raw eggs, so I'm never allowed to lick the mixing spoon. With these eggless brownies, I can lick the batter— yippie!! I was surprised how yummy these brownies are and how much they tasted like normal brownies."

MAKES ABOUT 30 KID-SIZED BROWNIES

2 tablespoons arrowroot powder

2 tablespoons cornstarch

4 tablespoons water

6 tablespoons unsalted butter (substitute a trans-fat-free nondairy margarine if allergic to dairy)

¾ cup semisweet chocolate chips (use non-dairy chocolate chips if allergic to dairy)

2 teaspoons pure vanilla extract

½ cup sugar

½ cup Purple Puree (see Make-Ahead Recipe #1, p. 43)

¼ cup plus 2 tablespoons Flour Blend (see Make-Ahead Recipe #10, p. 56)

¼ cup oat bran

1 tablespoon unsweetened cocoa powder

1 teaspoon instant coffee powder

¼ teaspoon *each* salt and cinnamon

Optional Extra Boost: 1 cup chopped walnuts

Powdered sugar, for dusting

Preheat oven to 350 degrees. Butter or spray only the bottom, not the sides, of an 8-inch or 9-inch square baking pan.

In a small bowl, completely dissolve the arrowroot and cornstarch in the water. Set aside. Melt the butter and chocolate chips together in a double boiler or metal bowl over simmering water (or in a microwave, checking every 15 seconds). Remove from heat and allow mixture to cool a bit. Meanwhile, in another bowl, stir the dissolved cornstarch mixture together with the vanilla, sugar, and Purple Puree. Combine this with the cooled chocolate mixture.

In a mixing bowl, whisk together the Flour Blend, oat bran, cocoa powder, coffee, salt, and cinnamon. Add this to the chocolate mixture and blend thoroughly. Mix in the chopped walnuts, if using, then pour the entire mixture into the baking pan.

Bake for 30 to 35 minutes, or until a toothpick comes out clean. Allow to cool completely in pan before cutting the brownies using a plastic or butter knife. Dust with powdered sugar, if desired.

Keeps for a week in the refrigerator, covered tightly.

PER SERVING (1 BROWNIE, 20G): *Calories 68; Total Fat 3.7g; Fiber 0.7g; Total Carbohydrates 9.2g; Sugars 6.0g; Protein .7g; Sodium 21mg; Cholesterol 6mg.* 26% less calories, 44% less fat, and 34% less cholesterol than traditional recipe.

Sneaky Chef
Classics

The following five recipes are adapted from my first book, *The Sneaky Chef: Simple Strategies for Hiding Healthy Foods in Kids' Favorite Meals*. No Sneaky Chef should be without these classic kid favorites. These are only a few of the foods that are on just about every kids' menu in restaurants across the country, so we know children adore them. I can virtually guarantee you that you won't have to fight to get your little ones to eat this food.

Battling 4 Hungry Boys Without Help!

A few days ago I tried my first "sneaky" recipe from my new cookbook, The Sneaky Chef by Missy Chase Lapine. We had two little boys over to play so I thought I'd slack off and make mac 'n' cheese for dinner. (Doug wasn't home and I wasn't about to battle four boys without help.)

I looked doubtfully at the cookbook, thinking it couldn't help me without a separate trip to the store, but was pleasantly surprised! There were actually a few suggestions for improving boxed mac 'n' cheese! The first was to add 2–4 tablespoons of White Bean Puree along with the regular cheese sauce package and just make it as directed. I looked up the recipe for White Bean Puree thinking it would be hard to make or I wouldn't have the ingredients. It said to mix a can of white beans (in a food processor if you've got one) with few tablespoons of water. That's it!

Easy enough. I keep canned beans in the pantry, so that was no problem. I blended them. I added a few tablespoons to the boxed mac 'n' cheese, and I served it. The kids loved it. They had no idea it was any different. But they got fiber, protein, whatchamacallit, and (probably) some vitamin . . . whatever. And they didn't even blink.

So I'm sold. I'm a believer. If I never try another recipe, it'll be worth keeping this book around!

Emily W., Misawa, Japan (mother of 3)
Adapted from www.actegratuit.blogspot.com

Quick Fixes for Boxed Mac 'n' Cheese

These quick fixes for boxed mac 'n' cheese have become a staple in American homes for parents who want to inject more nutrients into the convenience of the ever-popular boxed meal.

Each of the nutritional boosters listed here has been kid-tested and has proven to be undetectable in taste, texture, and color. Start by adding the least amount recommended of just one of the nutritional boosters listed below. Add a little more each time you serve this dish (which is served in our house virtually every day). You can also mix two or more of the boosters as long as the total is no more than about ½ cup total of puree per 6-ounce box of macaroni and cheese.

---

* 2 to 4 tablespoons White Bean Puree
   (See Make-Ahead Recipe #9, p. 54)

Prepare macaroni and cheese according to directions on package. Add White Bean Puree into the cheese sauce, mixing until well blended.

* 2 to 4 tablespoons White Puree
   (see Make-Ahead Recipe #4, p. 48)

Prepare macaroni and cheese according to directions on package. Add White Puree into the cheese sauce, mixing until well blended.

If sauce becomes too dry, simply add an extra tablespoon of milk and extra cheese.

* 2 to 4 tablespoons Orange Puree
   (See Make-Ahead Recipe #2, p. 44)

Prepare macaroni and cheese according to directions on package. Add Orange Puree into the cheese sauce, mixing until well blended. This one works best with an extra slice of American cheese or ¼ cup of grated cheddar melted into the sauce to help mask the carrots, which have a bit more distinguishable taste.

* ¼ cup to ½ cup tofu

Prepare macaroni and cheese according to directions on package. Puree tofu in a food processor until smooth or mash it well with the back of a fork. Add pureed tofu into the cheese sauce, mixing until well blended.

* 1 to 2 slices American cheese or
  ¼ cup grated cheddar cheese

Prepare macaroni and cheese according to directions on package. Add extra cheese to the packaged cheese sauce, mixing well until completely melted.

"I have been blending away for about six months now and have it so that my kids think that the mac 'n' cheese 'tastes funny' without the Orange Puree."

— Kathleen T., Lynnwood, WA (mother of 2)

Quick Fixes for Store-Bought Tomato Sauce

Each of the nutritional boosters below not only enhances the nutritional profile of your children's favorite bottled pasta sauce, but also helps to cut the acidity of the tomatoes, which may alleviate any upset stomach. Each booster has proven to be undetectable in taste, and any slight change in color can quickly be reversed by adding a little canned tomato paste. Start by adding the least amount recommended of just one of the following nutritional boosters. Add a little more each time you serve this sauce. You can also mix two or more of the boosters below, up to about ½ cup total per 1 cup of store-bought tomato sauce.

Each of the following quick fixes is for 1 cup of bottled sauce:

* 2 to 4 tablespoons White Bean Puree
   (See Make-Ahead Recipe #9, p. 54)
Combine White Bean Puree with store-bought sauce, mixing until well blended.

* 2 to 4 tablespoons White Puree
   (See Make-Ahead Recipe #4, p. 48)
Combine White Puree with store-bought sauce, mixing until well blended. If the sauce becomes too light, simply mix in a tablespoon or so of canned tomato paste to bring the color back to a deeper red.

* 2 to 4 tablespoons Orange Puree
   (See Make-Ahead Recipe #2, p. 44)
Combine Orange Puree with store-bought sauce, mixing until well blended. If the sauce becomes too light, simply mix in a tablespoon or so of canned tomato paste to bring the color back to a deeper red.

* ¼ cup evaporated milk

Combine evaporated milk with store-bought sauce, mixing until well blended. This makes more of a pink sauce.

"I definitely didn't used to have this much fun in the kitchen, but now we're all benefiting from the fruits and vegetables and I'm having a blast!"

—*Denise G. Bala Cynwyd, PA (mother of 2)*

Brainy Brownies

This is the signature recipe from the first Sneaky Chef *book. Everyone was amazed that no one—neither kids nor adults—could detect the hidden spinach, blueberries, oat bran, wheat germ, or the missing fat and sugar. I received feedback, however, that the pan size was too big for the quantity below, so I have modified the directions here.*

MAKES ABOUT 30 KID-SIZED BROWNIES

6 tablespoons unsalted butter

¾ cup semisweet chocolate chips

2 large eggs

2 teaspoons pure vanilla extract

½ cup sugar

½ cup Purple Puree (see Make-Ahead Recipe #1, p. 43)

¼ cup plus 2 tablespoons Flour Blend (see Make-Ahead Recipe #10, p. 56)

1 tablespoon unsweetened cocoa powder

¼ cup oat bran

¼ teaspoon salt

Optional Extra Boost: 1 cup chopped walnuts

Powdered sugar, for dusting

Preheat oven to 350 degrees. Butter or spray only the bottom, not the sides, of an 8-inch or 9-inch square baking pan.

Melt the butter and chocolate chips together in a double boiler or metal bowl over simmering water (or in a microwave, checking every 15 seconds). Remove from heat and allow mixture to cool a bit. Meanwhile, in another bowl, stir together the eggs, vanilla, sugar, and Purple Puree. Combine this purple egg mixture with the cooled chocolate mixture.

In a mixing bowl, stir together the Flour Blend, oat bran, cocoa powder, and salt. Add this to the chocolate mixture and blend thoroughly. Mix in the chopped walnuts, if using, then pour the entire mixture into the baking pan.

Bake for 30 to 35 minutes, or until a tooth-pick comes out clean. Allow to cool completely in pan. Dust with powdered sugar, if desired.

Keeps for a week in the refrigerator, covered tightly.

PER SERVING (1 BROWNIE, 21G): *Calories 67; Total Fat 4.0g; Fiber 0.6g; Total Carbohydrates 7.8g; Sugars 6.1g; Protein 1.0g; Sodium 26mg; Cholesterol 20mg.* 14% less fat, 24% less cholesterol, 33% less carbs, 142% more fiber, 45% less sodium, and 34% less sugars than traditional recipe.

Give That Recipe to the
Cafeteria Ladies!

Dear Sneaky Chef,

I make your Brainy Brownies often for my son (he's a first grader) to take to school for a snack. The kids are learning about making healthy choices and were asked not to bring in sweets for snack. Well, my kids help make the brownies, so they know what's in them. My son took two to school for snack the next day and got in an argument with some of his classmates because they thought he wasn't making a healthy choice! He told them that he knows they have healthy stuff like blueberries, spinach, and wheat germ because he helped make them. The other kids got excited that they could have brownies and still eat fruits and veggies! So my son comes homes and tells me that I need to give that recipe to the cafeteria ladies so that they can make them for the whole school so everyone can be healthy and still get brownies!

— Jodie C., Rochester, NY (mother of 2)

I've Done It!

I was skeptical at first, wondering how on earth I could disguise spinach in any food. But I've done it! My sneaky chocolate-chocolate chip cookies (with green vegetable puree) are now gone, and the chocolate chip cookies (with white bean puree) I made today were declared "Yummy." Last night I made chicken nuggets with hidden orange puree, and my very picky Ethan gobbled them up. I did not know the pleasure I would get from feeding my family a delicious and nutritious meal!

—Esther B., Marion, WI (mother of 3)
Adapted from www.EthanZachEmma.blogspot.com

Unbelievable Chocolate Chip Cookies

indulge   veggie   whole grains

These delicious cookies took the nation by storm after Al Roker and Natalie Morales happily munched on them before millions of Today Show *viewers in April 2007. People raved that unlike "normal" cookies, the whole grains and beans gave them some real staying power and didn't cause the usual sugar spike and crash that can accompany other sweets. I've revamped the classic recipe to omit almonds so these can be used in schools at bake sales. (No one's taking any chances since so many kids are allergic to nuts.) I've also substituted oat bran for ground oats because the bran is already a finer texture and adds more fiber. Since readers found the original cookies to be too small, I've made these cookies twice as large.*

MAKES ABOUT 4 DOZEN COOKIES

- 1 cup **Flour Blend** (see Make-Ahead Recipe #10, p. 56)
- ½ teaspoon baking soda
- ½ teaspoon salt
- ¼ cup oat bran
- 8 tablespoons unsalted butter, softened
- ¼ cup sugar
- ¼ cup brown sugar, packed

- 1 large egg
- 1 teaspoon pure vanilla extract
- ¼ cup **White Bean Puree** (see Make-Ahead Recipe #9, p. 54)
- ½ cup semisweet chocolate chips
- Optional Extra Boost: 1 cup chopped walnuts or dried berries such as blueberries or raisins

Preheat oven to 350 degrees.

In a large bowl, whisk together the Flour Blend, baking soda, salt, and oat bran. Set aside.

In the bowl of an electric mixer, beat butter and both sugars until creamy. Beat in egg, vanilla, and White Bean Puree. Add dry ingredients and mix on low speed. Stir in chocolate chips and walnuts or dried berries, if using. Make two-bite cookies by dropping rounded teaspoonfuls, spaced 2 inches apart, onto nonstick or parchment-lined baking sheets.

Bake for 12 to 14 minutes or until golden brown. Let cool on a metal rack.

Store cookies in airtight container for up to 3 days or freeze them in a plastic bag for up to 3 months.

PER SERVING (1 COOKIE, 21G): *Calories 46; Total Fat 2.6g; Fiber 0.5g; Total Carbohydrates 5.6g; Sugars 3.0g; Protein 0.8g; Sodium 37mg; Cholesterol 9mg.* 11% less calories, 10% less fat, 11% less carbs, 55% more fiber, 48% more potassium, 20% less sodium, 26% more protein, and 25% less sugars than traditional recipe.

The Cookies Have Helped!

Dear Ms. Sneaky,

My main reason for trying these cookies is to help with my daughter, Elizabeth. She suffers from pretty nasty headaches quite often. They make her sick. I think I may have narrowed down why she gets them. I think she might be hypoglycemic. Anyway, she seems to get the headaches when she hasn't eaten for a couple of hours. At school she has to make a special trip to the nurse's office for a snack each day to keep her levels high enough. Well, these cookies have some whole grains in them as well as beans. The combinations of the different ingredients will help her body burn things slowly. The cookies HAVE helped with Elizabeth's headaches and blood sugar levels!

Stephanie L., Buckeye, AZ (mother of 4)

(adapted from www.alittlebitofheaven.blogspot.com)

Crunchy Chicken Tenders

You can gradually increase the amount of Orange Puree used in this batter. Your kids may not be able to see the veggies under the crunchy breading, but their little bodies know the nutrients are there because, overall, they just feel more energized. You can pan-fry these in a little heart-healthy olive oil or oven bake them if you are short on time in the kitchen.

MAKES 4 TO 6 SERVINGS

1 pound boneless, skinless chicken tenders
(or boneless, skinless chicken breasts,
cut into strips)

¼ teaspoon salt

½ cup flour, ideally whole wheat

2 large eggs

¼ to ½ cup Orange Puree
(see Make-Ahead Recipe #2, p. 44)

2 cups Better Breading (see Make-Ahead
Recipe #12, p. 59)

½ cup grated Parmesan cheese

2 tablespoons olive oil, for pan-fry method

Season chicken tenders with salt. Place flour in a shallow dish or on a plate. Beat eggs with Orange Puree in a shallow bowl and place next to the flour. In a third shallow dish or on a paper plate, combine the Better Breading with the Parmesan cheese.

Dredge each piece of chicken in the flour, shaking off excess, then the egg mixture, and then the Better Breading mixture. Press the breading evenly onto both sides of the chicken. Put on waxed or parchment paper and store in the refrigerator for cooking tomorrow, or proceed to cook immediately.

Pan-fry method:

Heat 2 tablespoons oil in a large skillet over moderately high heat until hot but not smoking. Add a few strips at a time, pan-frying on one side until the crumbs look golden, about 2 to 3 minutes. Watch for burning, and turn down heat if necessary. With tongs, turn the pieces over and lightly brown the second side until golden, about 3 minutes. Reduce the heat to low and continue heating chicken until cooked through, about another 10 minutes. Blot cooked tenders on paper towels to remove excess oil.

Oven-bake method (not as brown and crisp, but quicker):

Preheat oven to 400 degrees.

Place breaded tenders on a cookie sheet lightly sprayed with oil and bake for 10 to 12 minutes. Turn chicken tenders over once with tongs, then return to oven for another 10 to 12 minutes until cooked through.

PER SERVING (167G): *Calories 329; Total Fat 8.0g; Fiber 5.1g; Total Carbohydrates 33.3g; Sugars 2.2g; Protein 31.2g; Sodium 540mg; Cholesterol 121mg.* 750% more fiber, 31% more potassium and 13% less sodium than traditional recipe.

Kids' Choice Nuggets

By the way, I recommend making the Sneaky Chef's Crunchy Chicken Tenders recipe. They are so delicious and crisp, and you can't even taste the sweet potatoes that they're made with. I told Brynlee she could have ANY meal of her choice for her birthday, and she chose these. They are the only chicken nugget recipe I'll ever make again!!

—Jennifer W.,
Farmington Mills, MI (mother of 2)
(adapted from
www.whitingfamily.blogspot.com)

Acknowledgments

At this point, I would like to acknowledge my readers because your passionate response to my books is so important to me. Your letters are my inspiration. I treasure your support and hope it will continue.

Creative development of a book involves teamwork. The team responsible for helping me is uniquely talented. My heartfelt thanks to—The Perseus Book Group/Running: CEO, David Steinberger; Executive Editor, Jennifer Kasius; Publisher, Jon Anderson; Associate Publisher, Craig Herman; Art Director, Bill Jones; Publicist, Melissa Appleby; and interior designer Alicia Freile; literary agents Joelle Delbourgo and Molly Lyons; Chef Tyler Florence; food photographer, Jerry Errico; food stylist, Brian Preston-Campbell; graphics designer Kris Weber of A/W Design; consultants Brigitte Miner, Laurence Chase, Karen Ganz, Carol Chase, and Sharon Hammer; and book consultant, Amanita Rosenbush.

You are the essence of our success.

Overall development of The Sneaky Chef brand is important as well. The following people are an integral part of bringing The Sneaky Chef into your homes: Brand Manager, Evan Morgenstein of PMG Chefs and his team Laura Cutler, Zach Nadler, and Raegan Herbert; licensing agent, Jonathan Close; Whole Foods Market team leaders Paul Koffa, Leigh DeNardo, and Paul Chan; Parenting Magazine editor-in-chief Susan Kane, and Deputy Editor Elizabeth Shaw; publicist Jennifer Prost; and Karen Wish and Tina Rosengarten of Morgan Stanley Children's Hospital of New York-Presbyterian.

Your genius brought The Sneaky Chef to life.

My family and friends are my support system. Thank you for your overall encouragement and confidence in me.

Finally, thank you Rick, Samantha and Emily. You are my world.

Dear Readers,

Thank you for sharing your time, ideas, and requests with us, and for making *The Sneaky Chef* a part of your life. To continue to share your ideas and comments, and for new recipes, tips, special promotions, and appearance dates, please visit us at:

www.TheSneakyChef.com

I also invite you to share your experience with this method and your own sneaky ideas by emailing me personally at **Missy@TheSneakyChef.com**. And you may also send me your own home video or CD of any Sneaky Chef moments—good or bad—and share how your family is doing. Send to:

The Sneaky Chef
PO Box 117
Ardsley on Hudson, NY 10503

As often as possible, I will upload these videos to my website, and my viewers can vote on which family will receive free personal coaching from me.

Index

Recipes Listed by Make-Ahead Ingredient